Worldwide Nude Horizons

The Best Naturist Vacations
Around the Globe

By
Victoria Collins

Worldwide Nude Horizons

The Best Naturist Vacations Around the Globe

Contents

Introduction

Imagine a travel experience that liberates the body, mind, and spirit—where the barriers of clothing are shed, and nature envelops you entirely. Welcome to the world of naturist travel, a journey that offers a profound sense of freedom, acceptance, and connection with the natural world and fellow travelers. This book sets out to be your comprehensive guide to exploring the most beautiful and liberating naturist destinations around the globe. Whether you're a seasoned naturist or just beginning to discover this unique lifestyle, our goal is to inspire and guide you to unforgettable experiences.

For many, the thought of naturist travel can be daunting and exhilarating in equal measure. Societal norms have long dictated our relationship with nudity, often relegating it to the realm of privacy and taboo. Yet, when practiced in a respectful and communal environment, naturism transcends these constraints, promoting body positivity, reducing stress, and fostering a stronger connection to the environment. This book invites you to step out of your comfort zone, embrace your natural self, and partake in an enriching vacation experience unlike any other. We have meticulously curated a list of destinations, practical advice, and cultural insights to ensure your journey is both comfortable and enlightening.

Naturism is more than just shedding your clothes; it's about shedding the constraints and expectations imposed by society. It's about connecting with nature on a deeper level, embracing your body just as it is, and respecting others who are doing the same. The philosophy of naturism encourages a life lived without artifice, where authenticity reigns. When you leave behind the trappings of modernity—even if just for a short while—you encounter a simpler, more genuine way of being. Imagine walking along a pristine beach with the sun warming your bare skin or hiking through secluded trails where the only sounds are the birds and the rustling leaves. This is the promise of naturist travel.

Embarking on this journey requires a touch of planning and a sense of adventure. Throughout these pages, we'll explore continents and cultures, giving you the necessary tools to navigate the legalities and etiquette of naturist environments. From bustling naturist resorts in North America to secluded beaches in the Caribbean, each destination offers its own unique flavor and opportunities for soulful rejuvenation. We've also included tips on what to pack, how to prepare mentally and physically, and how to make the most of your naturist excursions. This isn't just a guide; it's an invitation to open your mind and embark on a transformative adventure.

Our journey through naturist travel will help you discover the joys of baring all in destinations renowned for their natural beauty and welcoming atmospheres. In North America, naturist resorts offer a range of experiences, from social gatherings to serene hideaways. Picture yourself lounging beside a pool set against a backdrop of rugged mountains or joining a beachside volleyball game where fun takes precedence over formality. Travel a bit farther, and the Caribbean offers paradisiacal settings where azure waters and golden sands create the perfect canvas for naturist relaxation.

South America brings its own flair to the naturist landscape, with Brazil, Argentina, and Uruguay offering coastal retreats that blend Latin American culture with naturist principles. Western and Eastern Europe, too, present fascinating contrasts—from the sophisticated naturist capitals of France and Spain to the untamed beauty of Croatia and Bulgaria. Each destination not only promises breathtaking landscapes but also a cultural tapestry that enriches your naturist experience.

Of course, naturism isn't confined to the Western world. Mediterranean marvels await in Greece and Italy, while the Middle East and Africa offer emerging naturist scenes that are both exciting and unexpected. Asia, with its hidden paradises, and Oceania, with its casual, laid-back vibe, round out our global exploration. Naturist travel is, indeed, a universal language, one that transcends borders and unites people in a shared love of nature and authenticity.

Our commitment is to ensure that your naturist travels are not only liberating but also respectful of local customs and the environment. You'll find chapters dedicated to sustainable and ethical travel, wellness benefits associated with naturism, and how to make these experiences inclusive for families and solo travelers alike. Whether you're interested in the meditative practices of naturist yoga or the social vibrancy of group naturist trips, we've got you covered. Safety tips, accommodation insights, and festival guides further ensure that you have all the information you need at your fingertips.

One of the most thrilling aspects of naturist travel is its ever-evolving nature. The naturist community is continually discovering new destinations and creating innovative ways to experience this lifestyle. In our concluding chapters, we'll take a look at the future of naturist travel, exploring emerging locations and trends that push the boundaries of what we thought possible. From adventurous naturist cruises to eco-resorts designed to leave no footprint, the horizons are broadening, offering even more ways to experience naturism.

Ultimately, naturist travel is about freedom—freedom from societal expectations, freedom to connect deeply with the natural world, and freedom to embrace your own authenticity. This book aims to be your faithful companion on this voyage, offering guidance, inspiration, and practical advice as you explore some of the most beautiful naturist destinations on Earth. Whether you're traveling with family, friends, as a couple, or even solo, there's a world of naturist adventures waiting for you.

So, let's cast aside conventional limitations and set forth on a journey that promises not just travel, but transformation. Welcome to the liberating world of naturist travel. We're excited to be a part of your journey, guiding you to experiences that celebrate nature, freedom, and the simple joy of being.

Chapter 1:
The Allure of Naturist Travel

The allure of naturist travel lies in the extraordinary sense of freedom and connection it brings, both to nature and oneself. Imagine the sun's warmth on bare skin, the gentle touch of the ocean's waves, and the liberating absence of clothing—all contributing to an unmatched feeling of serenity and authenticity. For the seasoned traveler or the curious newcomer to naturism, this unique way of experiencing the world promises much more than just a break from the everyday grind. It offers a chance to reshape one's relationship with the body and the environment, embracing a lifestyle that prioritizes well-being and natural beauty. Be it the tranquil beaches of Europe, the lush retreats in South America, or the vibrant communities in North America, naturist destinations are calling out to those who seek an adventure that's as exhilarating as it is grounding. So why not let go of the ordinary and step into a realm where the world's most beautiful landscapes meet the most genuine version of yourself?

Understanding Naturism

Naturism, often referred to as nudism, is more than just the practice of being nude. It is a philosophy and lifestyle that champions the belief in living in harmony with nature, promoting self-respect, respect for others, and a deep sense of freedom and liberation. Adopting this way of life can unlock a world of experiences that intertwine physical freedom with emotional and mental wellness.

The origins of naturism trace back to various ancient civilizations where nudity was viewed as a natural state of being and an expression of oneness with nature. While the modern naturist movement began to take shape in Europe in the early 20th century, it has since spread worldwide, resonating with those seeking a more relaxed and natural way of life.

For many, naturism is about reclaiming the body's natural state and breaking away from the social conventions and pressures of modern society. The allure lies in the simplicity and authenticity it offers, stripping away the pretenses we often build up. Being nude amongst fellow naturists fosters a sense of equality and genuine connection, as clothing often signifies various forms of social and economic status.

As you explore naturist travel, it's important to recognize that naturism is underpinned by principles of mutual respect and non-judgment. This philosophy encourages individuals to embrace their bodies, imperfections and all, fostering a positive self-image and acceptance of themselves and others. The feeling of the sun on your skin, the breeze as it dances across your body, and the connection to the earth underfoot can be incredibly freeing and deeply rejuvenating.

Naturist destinations worldwide often reflect the values of this lifestyle. Beaches with pristine sands, forests rich with flora, and serene lakesides become the idyllic settings where naturists can feel at one with their environment. These places often come with a sense of sanctuary, buffered from the inquisitive gaze of the non-naturist world, providing a safe space to unwind and feel unfettered.

Exploring naturist venues also means adhering to a certain etiquette that ensures everyone's comfort and safety. Respecting personal space, refraining from overt behavior, and maintaining a friendly and non-invasive demeanor are cornerstones of naturist interaction. It's an unwritten code designed to foster respect, comfort, and a shared sense of community.

In a world rife with digital distractions and endless to-do lists, naturism offers an antidote: the chance to slow down and reconnect with what it truly means to exist in the moment. For many, naturist vacations are less about the destination and more about the journey—of discovering a new sense of self, unburdened by societal expectations and constraints.

Families, too, find value in naturist experiences, as they offer a wholesome and nurturing environment for children to grow up learning body positivity and respect for others. Watching a sunset over a naturist beach with your loved ones, feeling the sheer joy of splashing in the ocean, together without the barrier of clothing, creates lasting memories and strengthens familial bonds.

In addition to the communal and emotional benefits, naturism can be a great boost to personal health. Naturist activities like yoga, hiking, and swimming are done in the nude, which can feel more natural and invigorating. The physical sensation of freedom allows for greater relaxation and enhances the mindfulness one can achieve while engaging in these activities.

For those interested in diving into the naturist lifestyle, beginning your journey with naturist travel can be an excellent choice. Numerous resorts, beaches, parks, and cruise lines are dedicated to offering naturist-friendly environments. These spaces are designed to make newcomers feel welcome and to provide experienced naturists with the comforts and amenities they enjoy.

Understanding naturism also involves recognizing its variations across different cultures. While some places have longstanding naturist traditions, in others, the movement is slowly gaining traction. Each destination offers its own unique take on naturism, reflecting local customs and societal norms. These cultural nuances add richness and diversity to the global naturist community.

As we move forward in this book, you'll learn about the best naturist destinations across different continents. From the lush landscapes of South America to the historic and sophisticated regions of Western Europe, each location offers a unique opportunity to practice naturism in a setting that enhances the experience. Whether you're drawn to the serene beaches of the Caribbean or the secluded retreats of Oceania, there's a naturist destination out there waiting to be discovered.

Understanding naturism is the first step towards embracing this liberating lifestyle. It's about more than shedding clothes—it's about shedding societal pressures, embracing authenticity, and finding a deeper connection with the world around you. As you embark on your naturist travel adventures, remember that each step you take helps you become more grounded, more free, and more in touch with your natural self.

The journey into naturism is a deeply personal one, filled with discovery, connection, and a renewed appreciation for the natural world. Whether you're a seasoned naturist or just beginning to explore this way of life, there's no doubt that naturist travel can offer some of the most rewarding and unforgettable experiences you'll ever have.

So, with an open mind and a spirit ready for adventure, let's journey into the world of naturism and witness firsthand the beauty and liberation that it brings.

Benefits of Going Nude

The allure of naturist travel goes beyond the simple thrill of sunbathing in the buff. For many, naturism is a deeply fulfilling lifestyle that offers a unique path to personal liberation, self-acceptance, and genuine connection with nature. Let's dive into the myriad benefits that going nude brings, making naturist travel an unforgettable, life-changing experience.

One of the most compelling benefits of naturism is the profound sense of liberation. Stripping away clothes metaphorically allows you to shed societal expectations and pressures. The simple act of being naked restores a childlike freedom, rejuvenating your spirit. In naturist environments, social hierarchies based on appearance, fashion, or status dissolve. You're left with a charming sense of equality and authenticity that is increasingly rare in our fast-paced, image-conscious society.

Naturism also offers unparalleled physical comfort. Think about those hot summer days when clothes stick to your skin, causing discomfort and irritation. Now picture yourself free from all that. The sun on your bare skin, the cool breeze, and the refreshing feeling of water against your whole body make tactile experiences infinitely more pleasurable. Your skin breathes easier, reducing the risk of skin issues associated with tight or non-breathable fabrics. It's not just about comfort; it's about enhancing your overall wellbeing.

On a deeper level, naturism fosters body positivity and self-acceptance. In a world inundated with unrealistic body standards, baring it all in a supportive, non-judgmental setting can be liberating. It allows you to confront and dismantle insecurities, fostering a profound respect for your own body. Seeing the diversity of shapes, sizes, and imperfections around you reinforces the beauty of human variety, helping you to appreciate your unique form. This newfound self-confidence is often carried back into your clothed life, enriching your self-esteem and interpersonal relationships.

Naturist travel also brings you closer to nature, revitalizing a primal connection that many have lost in urban settings. The tactile sensation of walking on sandy beaches, the feeling of grass underfoot, or the embrace of ocean waves against your skin reawaken your sensory experiences. This more intimate connection with your surroundings is grounding, offering a peaceful escape from the digital, disconnected world we often inhabit. You become more attuned to the rhythms of the natural world, finding tranquility and rejuvenation.

Socially, naturism can be transformative. Unlike most social settings, naturist environments encourage genuine interactions. Conversations flow more freely when stripped of social markers that typically dictate behavior. This openness fosters deep, meaningful connections and friendships based on mutual respect and shared experiences. Naturist communities are often tight-knit, welcoming newcomers with open arms and fostering a sense of belonging that's heartwarming and rare.

For those traveling with partners, naturism can add a layer of romanticism to your relationship. Sharing the vulnerability and intimacy of being nude strengthens bonds, encouraging trust and deep connection. It provides a unique vulnerability, stripping away pretense and inviting honest, open communication. Couples often find that they grow closer, creating cherished memories of shared liberation and joy.

Another often overlooked benefit of naturism is its potential for mental well-being. Being in a naturist setting promotes mindfulness, encouraging you to be present in the moment. Stripped of distractions like fashion trends or societal norms, you can fully engage with your surroundings and experiences. This heightened state of awareness can reduce stress, improve mood, and even foster creativity, offering a natural sanctuary for mental rejuvenation.

Furthermore, naturist travel can be an educational experience for both adults and children. It provides an opportunity to learn about the human body in a healthy, respectful context, fostering a positive attitude towards nudity and sexuality. This educational aspect is particularly valuable for families, teaching body positivity and respect for oneself and others from a young age. Children learn to see the human body as natural and normal, promoting a healthy self-image and reducing stigma.

Environmental consciousness is another cornerstone of naturism. Many naturist spaces emphasize sustainability, encouraging eco-friendly practices like recycling, conservation, and a minimalistic approach. This environmental ethos often inspires naturists to adopt similar practices in their own lives, fostering a broader impact on ecological sustainability. By reconnecting with nature in such an intimate way, individuals become more invested in protecting the environment, leading to more conscious travel choices.

Economically, naturist destinations often promote local businesses and communities. Many naturist resorts and campsites are family-owned, offering an authentically local experience. By choosing these destinations, you're supporting the local economy and helping to preserve unique cultural traditions. This economic benefit extends not just to the naturist spots themselves, but also to surrounding areas, creating a ripple effect that promotes regional growth and sustainability.

Lastly, naturist travel is often more straightforward and free from the complications of fashion and packing. Without the need for extensive wardrobes, your travel becomes lighter and more focused on the experience itself rather than material concerns. Packing becomes a breeze, focusing only on essentials and allowing you to travel more freely and spontaneously. This simplicity dovetails perfectly with the overarching ethos of naturism: living a life unencumbered by unnecessary baggage, both physical and metaphorical.

In conclusion, the benefits of going nude are as diverse and enriching as the naturist locations you'll discover. From physical comfort and mental well-being to profound social connections and environmental consciousness, naturism offers a holistic approach to travel and living. Whether you're a seasoned naturist or a curious newcomer, embracing nudity can profoundly impact your life, providing priceless experiences and lifelong memories. Ready to explore? The world of naturist travel awaits, promising journeys that transform far beyond the surface.

Chapter 2:
Preparing for Your Naturist Adventure

Embarking on a naturist adventure demands careful preparation to ensure a seamless and liberating experience. Begin by selecting lightweight, breathable clothing for your travels to the destination, yet remember that packing a sarong or quick-dry towel will be more practical than your usual bulky beach attire. Don't forget essential items like sunblock, insect repellent, and reusable water bottles, as staying hydrated and protected is key to comfort. Acquaint yourself with the legalities and cultural norms of your chosen locations, as these vary significantly around the globe, affecting how you'll conduct yourself in public spaces. Understanding and respecting local etiquette will not only help you avoid any awkward situations but also enrich your overall experience by fostering connections with locals and fellow travelers. Ready yourself emotionally and mentally as well; embrace the freedom that comes with shedding societal norms along with your clothes, and let the natural world rejuvenate your spirit as you embark on this unforgettable journey.

Packing Essentials

Embarking on a naturist adventure can be exhilarating, but like any trip, the success of your experience heavily depends on how well you prepare. When it comes to packing for a naturist vacation, the concept might seem simpler given the lack of clothing required. However, there's more to it than just leaving your wardrobe behind. Packing the right essentials not only ensures comfort and convenience but also enhances the quality of your naturist experience.

First and foremost, let's talk about clothing. Yes, you will need some! Even at the most liberating naturist resorts and beaches, there are moments when clothing is required—be it for meals, non-naturist excursions, or colder evenings. Opt for lightweight, breathable fabrics. Think loose-fitting sundresses, sarongs, kaftans, and shorts. These items are perfect for slipping on and off as needed, respecting the varying norms and regulations at different destinations.

A high-quality, wide-brimmed hat and a pair of good sunglasses are also indispensable. Naturist locations often bask in ample sunlight, and while the freedom to bare all is delightful, protecting your skin and eyes from harmful UV rays is crucial. Choose a hat that offers substantial coverage for your face, neck, and shoulders. A pair of polarized sunglasses will not only shield your eyes but also enhance your comfort during those sunlit strolls along the beach.

No naturist packing checklist would be complete without sunscreen, and copious amounts of it. Opt for a broad-spectrum, water-resistant sunscreen with a high SPF rating. Naturist vacations offer more skin exposure than typical holidays, making effective sun protection non-negotiable. Pack enough to last the duration of your trip and apply it liberally and frequently. Remember to pay extra attention to areas that aren't typically exposed to sun in your daily routine.

A beach bag is another essential. Choose one that's spacious and easy to carry, capable of holding all your day-trip necessities like sunscreen, a reusable water bottle, a foldable mat or towel, a book, and some snacks. Opt for waterproof materials to prevent your belongings from getting wet or damaged by sand.

Speaking of towels, bring more than one. Naturist resorts often have strict hygiene policies requiring the use of a personal towel when sitting or lying on shared surfaces. Invest in lightweight, quick-drying towels to keep them fresh and transportable. One for the beach, one for showering, and possibly another for general use around your accommodation should cover most of your needs.

Footwear might seem trivial on a naturist vacation, but it still matters. A pair of comfortable sandals or flip-flops is usually sufficient for the warm weather locations typical of naturist destinations. However, if your adventure includes any hiking or exploring rugged terrains, pack a pair of sturdy walking shoes.

Don't forget about the practicalities of personal care. Your regular toiletries are a given, but consider the naturist context. Bring biodegradable soap and shampoo to minimize your environmental footprint, especially if you're visiting eco-sensitive areas. If staying in a more secluded or rustic environment, a compact first-aid kit is indispensable. Include bandages, antiseptic wipes, insect repellent, and any medications you might need.

For those who enjoy documenting their travels, consider investing in a waterproof camera or protective case for your phone. Many naturist destinations feature stunning natural beauty, from crystal-clear waters to lush landscapes. Capture these moments safely without the risk of water damage to your devices.

Moreover, a small, lightweight backpack or cross-body bag for day trips is practical for carrying essentials without burdening yourself. It frees your hands and ensures you're prepared for excursions, hikes, or just a day trip to a nearby town.

Though it might not be the first thing that comes to mind, consider packing a small amount of laundry detergent. Being able to hand-wash clothing or towels can be a lifesaver, particularly for extended stays where laundry facilities aren't readily available.

Finally, embrace the opportunity for some digital downtime. While your phone and gadgets are essential for communication and capturing memories, take this chance to connect deeper with nature and yourself. Pack a good book, travel journal, or some art supplies. Engaging in these reflective activities can make your trip even more enriching.

Packing for a naturist adventure strikes a unique balance between minimalism and practicality. The essentials listed here aim to ensure that your focus remains on liberation and relaxation, without compromising on comfort and readiness for all scenarios. Embrace the simplicity—after all, that's a significant part of the naturist ethos.

With these packing essentials in your arsenal, you can look forward to a naturist journey that's as stress-free and satisfying as possible, ready to immerse yourself fully in the liberating experiences that await.

Navigating Legalities and Etiquette

Embarking on a naturist adventure can be one of the most liberating and unique travel experiences you'll ever have. However, like any other form of travel, it comes with its own set of rules and customs that you should be aware of to ensure a respectful and enjoyable journey. Understanding the legalities and etiquette surrounding naturism is crucial not only for your comfort but also for maintaining harmony with the communities you visit.

First and foremost, it's essential to understand that the legal stance on naturism can vary dramatically from country to country and even within regions of the same country. In some places, naturism is embraced with open arms, while in others, it can be severely restricted or outright illegal. To navigate these legalities, thorough research is your best ally. Before arriving at your destination, consult trusted sources such as local naturist associations, tourism boards, and online forums. These can provide updated legal information, helping you avoid any unpleasant encounters.

When in doubt, it's always wise to err on the side of caution. Even in destinations known for their naturist-friendly policies, specific venues, events, or times might have different rules. For example, certain beaches might be designated as clothing-optional only during certain hours of the day. Ignorance of these nuanced rules can lead to misunderstandings or even legal trouble. Therefore, being informed and respectful of local laws is not just courteous—it's essential.

Equally as important as understanding the legal landscape is adhering to proper naturist etiquette. Naturist etiquette is fundamentally about respect—for yourself, others, and the environment. While the norms may slightly differ depending on where you go, a few universal principles apply across the board.

One of the primary tenets of naturist etiquette is consent. Naturist spaces, though free-spirited, are not free-for-alls. Always seek consent before engaging in conversations or activities with others. What might seem like a friendly gesture in everyday settings can be misinterpreted in a naturist context. Consent ensures that everyone feels comfortable and respected, which contributes to a positive communal atmosphere.

Photography is another sensitive area in naturist environments. While your instinct might be to capture the beautiful moments and scenery, remember that people in naturist spaces value their privacy deeply. Always ask for permission before taking any photos, even if the individuals are not the primary subjects. Many naturist destinations enforce strict no-photography policies to safeguard the privacy of their guests. Ignoring these policies can lead to fines or expulsion from the venue, so it's best to be mindful.

Respecting personal space is also crucial. Even though naturism promotes a sense of community and shared experience, people have different comfort levels when it comes to physical proximity. Keep a considerate distance unless you're invited to come closer. This small consideration can go a long way in making everyone feel at ease.

Another key aspect of naturist etiquette involves the use of facilities and communal areas. Naturist resorts, beaches, and parks often provide amenities like pools, saunas, and lounges. When using these areas, always sit on a towel. This is not just for hygiene but also considered a sign of respect. Additionally, be mindful of your conversations and behavior, as loud or inappropriate actions can disturb others who are there to relax and enjoy the serene environment.

Environmental respect is another core principle of naturist etiquette. Naturism inherently entails a deep appreciation for nature, and this philosophy extends to how we treat the natural surroundings. Always clean up after yourself, avoid using single-use plastics, and support eco-friendly practices. By doing so, you help preserve these beautiful locations for future naturists to enjoy.

It's also noteworthy that naturism often intersects with local customs and traditions. In some cultures, nudity is more acceptable than in others. Being attuned to these cultural sensitivities is important. For instance, in many Western European countries, naturism is widely accepted and integrated into mainstream culture. On the other hand, in more conservative societies, public nudity is frowned upon, and even private naturist venues may have stricter codes of conduct.

Your demeanor and attitude also play a significant role in bridging these cultural nuances. Approach your naturist adventure with an open mind and a humble spirit. Show genuine interest in understanding the cultural context you're in. Politeness and adaptability are invaluable traits that can help you blend in seamlessly and enrich your experience.

Understanding these dynamics helps you navigate your naturist adventure smoothly. This awareness allows you to enjoy the freedom and thrill of naturism while fostering respect and understanding with the host communities and fellow travelers. Your conscientiousness not only enhances your experience but also contributes positively to the reputation of naturism as a respectful and meaningful way to travel.

Lastly, while naturism is very much about personal freedom and expression, it's essential to remember that it functions within a community. Contributing to this community in positive ways—whether by participating in local activities, sharing insights with fellow travelers, or simply being a respectful guest—can make your naturist adventure more impactful. Gratitude, kindness, and respect can transform a mere trip into a deeply fulfilling experience.

In conclusion, navigating the legalities and etiquette of naturist travel involves a blend of research, mindfulness, and respect. By understanding the laws, respecting personal boundaries, and embracing the shared values of the naturist community, you set the stage for a rewarding and harmonious adventure. As you prepare to explore the world's most beautiful naturist destinations, let these principles guide you, fostering not only a personal sense of freedom but also contributing to a larger culture of respect and appreciation.

Chapter 3:
North America's Best Naturist Destinations

In North America, naturism unveils a diverse spectrum of breathtaking landscapes and vibrant communities that welcome you to shed your inhibitions and embrace nature in its purest form. From the sun-drenched shores of California and Florida to the picturesque woodlands of British Columbia and Quebec, these destinations offer a magical blend of freedom, connection, and beauty. Imagine the soft sand beneath your feet on hidden beaches in Mexico or the serene surroundings of a pristine lake in Ontario. Each locale not only provides a chance to bask in the natural world without barriers but also an opportunity to connect with like-minded travelers who share your passion for uninhibited exploration. The essence of these destinations extends beyond physical liberation; it invites you to rediscover yourself and the world around you through the lens of naturism. North America's naturist hotspots are more than just vacation spots—they are sanctuaries of freedom, where every moment becomes a celebration of the human spirit and the beauty of our natural world.

USA Naturist Resorts

Scattered across the vast and varied landscapes of the United States, naturist resorts offer unique havens where you can embrace the liberating spirit of nudism in a diverse array of settings. From the sun-kissed beaches of Florida and California to the serene wooded retreats in the Midwestern heartland, each resort brings its own flavor of naturist freedom. Discover upscale resorts with luxurious amenities, rustic campsites that invite you to reconnect with nature, and vibrant communal spaces perfect for socializing and forming lifelong bonds. Whether relaxing by a crystal-clear pool, hiking nude trails, or participating in community events, these resorts provide the perfect backdrop for a memorable and freeing vacation. With a warm, welcoming atmosphere and a rich tapestry of destinations, USA naturist resorts promise an inspiring escape that nurtures both body and soul.

East Coast Gems showcase some of the best naturist resorts in the USA, offering a picturesque blend of coastline beauty and hospitable retreats where freedom and nature harmoniously coexist. These destinations are not just about sunbathing under the open sky; they're about embracing the ethos of naturism, which promotes respect for oneself, others, and the environment. From the golden sands of Florida to the rocky shores of Maine, the East Coast is dotted with naturist spots that cater to both the uninitiated and the seasoned naturist.

Florida, often dubbed as the sunshine state, is home to some of the most well-known and loved naturist resorts. For instance, *Haulover Beach* near Miami isn't just a sun worshipper's paradise but also a vibrant community where nudity is celebrated. It's one of the few places in the region where it's not only legal but also encouraged to ditch your swimsuit and revel in the sunshine. The clear, warm waters and the friendly atmosphere make it a perfect getaway for those looking to dip their toes—figuratively and literally—into the world of naturism.

Further north, nestled away from the bustling city life, lies *Sunsport Gardens* Family Naturist Resort in Loxahatchee Groves. This resort stands out for its commitment to family-friendly naturism, creating a safe and welcoming environment where all ages can freely express themselves. Activities abound, from yoga sessions to nature walks, making it a holistic retreat. It's a place where the philosophy of naturism is lived daily, fostering a sense of community and acceptance.

Another gem hidden in the East Coast's crown is *Gunnison Beach* in New Jersey. Located in the Sandy Hook area, it's the only legal clothing-optional beach in the state. Known for its breathtaking views of the New York City skyline, Gunnison Beach offers a unique blend of urban proximity and serene naturist freedom. The beach attracts a diverse crowd, from locals to tourists, all drawn by the allure of shedding societal barriers and embracing a more natural state of being.

Further up the coastline, Maine's natural charm isn't lost on naturists. Tucked away in Pownal lies the *Sunrise Acres Campground*, a lesser-known but equally enchanting naturist destination. Enveloped by pristine forests and meandering trails, it offers a secluded retreat where naturists can reconnect with nature in its purest form. Whether you're setting up camp or just spending a day, the tranquility and beauty of this place are undeniable, offering a peaceful escape from the everyday hustle.

In Vermont, the *Abbott's Glen* Naturist Resort exudes rustic elegance. Set amidst the picturesque New England landscapes, this resort is a haven for those seeking a blend of comfort and nature. Activities range from cozy bonfires to invigorating river swims, each moment designed to deepen your connection with nature. The resort is particularly noted for its exceptional hospitality, making every guest feel immediately at home.

Meanwhile, *Solair Family Nudist Resort* in Connecticut is another must-visit for those exploring the East Coast. Its origins date back to the 1930s, making it a cornerstone of naturist tradition in the region. With its various recreational activities, from hiking to tennis, and amenities like a crystal-clear lake and a clubhouse, Solair provides an enriching experience for naturists. It's not merely a resort, but a community where lifelong friendships are forged over shared values and mutual respect.

North Carolina offers its own unique slice of naturist bliss at the *Bar-S-Ranch*. A sprawling 400-acre property enveloped in nature's finest, it boasts an array of facilities including a large pool, hiking trails, and even a disc golf course. The resort prides itself on being not just a naturist destination but a sanctuary where naturists can rediscover the joys of outdoor life in their most natural state.

Heading up to Massachusetts, *Sandy Terraces* nudist campground provides a tranquil getaway for naturists in the Cape Cod area. This small, intimate campground offers a refuge from the hectic pace of modern life, allowing visitors to unwind and immerse themselves in the surrounding natural beauty. The charm of Sandy Terraces lies not just in its idyllic setting but in its warm, welcoming community where everyone is encouraged to connect and share their experiences.

For naturists craving a picturesque rural escape, Maryland's *Pine Tree Associates* presents an inviting option. This members-only club provides a luxuriant, wooded sanctuary with a welcoming atmosphere. Its seasonal activities, ranging from swimming in the pool to volleyball, encourage a vibrant yet relaxed community spirit. It's a place where naturist principles are lived fully, emphasizing wellness and environmental respect.

As you journey through these East Coast gems, it's evident that each destination possesses its own unique allure. Whether it's the family-friendly environment at Sunsport Gardens or the rustic charm of Abbott's Glen, there's an abundance of experiences waiting to be uncovered. These places exemplify the breadth and richness of naturist philosophy, offering spaces where freedom, respect, and nature converge harmoniously.

So, whether you're lounging on the sandy beaches of Florida, hiking through Vermont's picturesque landscapes, or discovering the tranquil corners of Maine, the East Coast promises an enlightening journey into naturism. Each destination invites you to leave behind the constraints of daily life, embrace the liberating ethos of naturism, and experience the world in a refreshingly natural way. Dive in, explore, and find your own slice of naturist paradise along this vibrant and undulating coastline.

West Coast Wonders

Cascading down the Pacific edge, the West Coast boasts a tapestry of wild coastal beauty, vibrant naturist communities, and a liberating spirit that calls to those seeking a free-spirited escape. From the sun-kissed shores of Southern California to the rugged coastline of Washington, this region is a goldmine for naturist enthusiasts looking to immerse themselves in nature while embracing the unobstructed freedom of the human form.

Starting in Southern California, there's a unique blend of urban flair and natural splendor that makes it a hit among naturists. San Diego, in particular, is home to the iconic Black's Beach. Behind the backdrop of striking cliffs, this expansive stretch of sand allows for a perfectly private and invigorating nude experience. While accessing it may require a bit of a hike, the journey itself is part of the adventure. Traversing steep trails and descending rugged paths, the arrival at Black's Beach feels like reaching a hidden paradise known only to those willing to seek it.

Further up the coast, the artistic enclave of San Francisco offers not just culture and history, but also the sanctuary of Baker Beach. Nestled beneath the majestic Golden Gate Bridge, this beach is famed for its welcoming naturist section at the north end. The exhilarating feeling of standing unencumbered with the bridge's red spires framing the horizon is immeasurable. It's a blend of freedom and grandeur, making Baker Beach more than just a naturist location—it's a symbol of bold liberation against an iconic American backdrop.

The journey through West Coast Wonders isn't complete without a stop at the stunning Oregon coastline. The state is celebrated for its natural beauty and progressive attitudes, which extend to its beach regulations. While many beaches in Oregon welcome naturists, Collins Beach on Sauvie Island is especially noteworthy. Just a short drive from Portland, this scenic spot along the Columbia River is favored for its serene atmosphere and the friendly community of naturists who frequent it. Its sheltered shores also provide the perfect setting for sunbathing, swimming, and spontaneous gatherings under the vast, open sky.

As one moves further north into Washington, the landscape begins to shift to dramatic cliffs, moss-laden forests, and crystal-clear waters. A crowning jewel of Washington's naturist spots is the aptly named Denny-Blaine Park in Seattle. This charming urban hideaway offers seclusion while still being in proximity to the city's artistic and culinary delights. Nestled along Lake Washington, this small waterfront park promotes a relaxed, clothing-optional atmosphere that attracts both locals and travelers alike. The tranquil waters and panoramic views create a serene environment ideal for those wanting to unwind and reconnect with nature.

Yet, beyond the beaches and parks, the West Coast also infuses naturism into its lifestyle, offering various events and community gatherings that celebrate this way of living. Southern California's annual World Naked Bike Ride and the numerous nude yoga classes available in cities such as Los Angeles and San Francisco mark just a few examples. These experiences foster a sense of unity and shared purpose among participants, who come together to advocate for body positivity and environmental awareness.

Camping also plays a pivotal role in the naturist experience along the West Coast. For those looking to combine the thrill of outdoor adventure with the freedom of naturist living, campsites like Lupin Lodge in Los Gatos, California, and Squaw Mountain Ranch in Estacada, Oregon, provide idyllic escapes. These retreats offer trails for hiking and biking, communal activities, and, most importantly, the joyful camaraderie of a like-minded community. The enveloping embrace of wilderness and the absence of daily stressors make for a rejuvenating retreat that nourishes both the body and the spirit.

Beyond the natural and communal aspects, the West Coast is interspersed with luxurious resorts and retreats that cater specifically to naturists. These havens offer amenities ranging from thermal springs and massage therapies to gourmet dining and wellness workshops. In the heart of the Napa Valley, The Willows secluded naturist retreat offers a blend of luxury and tranquility surrounded by sprawling vineyards and lush landscapes, whereas Northern California's Mountain Air Ranch combines rustic charm with comfort, providing a welcome escape into serene woodlands.

Lastly, the burgeoning naturist scene along the West Coast extends into Canada, where British Columbia offers breathtaking naturist locales like Wreck Beach in Vancouver. Just north of the border, this expansive beach is renowned for its vibrant, welcoming community and stunning views of the Pacific Ocean. Wreck Beach embodies the true spirit of naturism, with its diverse crowd and festive atmosphere making it a beloved destination for naturists from both sides of the border.

The allure of the West Coast for naturists lies not only in its natural beauty but in the shared ethos of freedom, acceptance, and connection with the environment. Whether it's the thrill of exploring a secluded beach, the camaraderie found at a naturist camp, or the relaxation of an upscale resort, the West Coast promises a journey of self-discovery and boundless liberation for every naturist enthusiast.

Canada Naturist Hotspots

Canada offers a wealth of evocative naturist destinations that harmonize with its breathtaking natural beauty. From the rugged coastlines of British Columbia to the quaint charm of Quebec, each province brings its unique flair to the naturist experience. Picture yourself unwinding at Wreck Beach in Vancouver, a stunning stretch where forest meets the ocean, creating an idyllic scene for complete liberation. Or perhaps venture to Quebec, where Oka National Park invites you to bask in serenity amidst lush greenery and soft sands. These Canadian hotspots are not just places to shed your clothes but also sanctuaries that allow you to connect deeply with nature's profound tranquility.

British Columbia Beauty

It's hard to rival the spectacular landscapes and serene ambiance of British Columbia. Nestled on the west coast of Canada, this region offers a perfect blend of majestic mountains, verdant forests, and serene coastlines, making it an ideal backdrop for naturist adventures. Whether you're an experienced naturist or just beginning your journey, British Columbia promises an unparalleled experience of freedom and connection with nature.

Start your exploration in Vancouver, a bustling city cradled by mountains and ocean. While you might associate Vancouver with urban sophistication, it's also a gateway to some of the most scenic naturist spots. Wreck Beach, located near the University of British Columbia, is a renowned naturist beach that stretches over 4.8 kilometers. It's not just a place to shed your clothes; it's a community. Summer weekends bring together locals and travelers drawn by the beach's inclusive and vibrant atmosphere. The backdrop of coastal rainforest and the scent of salt air make it a haven for those seeking both relaxation and invigoration.

As you venture further into British Columbia, the landscape transforms into sprawling vineyards and rolling hills. The Okanagan Valley, famous for its wineries, is also home to the naturist resort, CottonTail Corner. Here, naturism is synonymous with wellness. You can spend your days tasting world-class wines, wandering through lush vineyards, and soaking up the sun by Lake Okanagan. The resort provides an oasis where you can truly unwind, away from the hustle and bustle.

Journeying to Vancouver Island reveals even more scenic delights. The island is a treasure trove of naturist spots, each offering unique experiences. Little Tribune Bay on Hornby Island is a must-visit, known for its tranquil waters and soft sand. The bay's seclusion offers a sense of privacy, making it perfect for naturism. Imagine spending your afternoons kayaking through the crystal-clear waters or exploring hidden coves, all in the comfort of your natural state.

Closer to the island's urban center, Victoria, lies another gem: Thetis Lake. The lake is a local favorite for naturist swimming and sunbathing. Surrounded by forested areas, it provides a delightful escape where you can immerse yourself in nature. The trails circling the lake are perfect for refreshing walks, and you might spot local wildlife, adding an element of adventure to your naturist experience.

British Columbia's rugged interior offers yet another facet of its natural beauty. The Kootenay region, with its picturesque mountains and serene lakes, is ideal for those who crave adventure. Nakusp Hot Springs, located in the heart of the Kootenays, offers natural hot pools in a forested setting. These springs have attracted naturists for years, thanks to their tranquil ambiance and healing waters. There's something profoundly liberating about lounging in warm, mineral-rich water, surrounded by towering pines and the sound of bird song.

Even the more remote areas of British Columbia hold naturist treasures. Savary Island, often referred to as the "Hawaii of the North," is accessible only by boat. This island boasts sandy beaches and warm waters. South Beach, in particular, is a favored spot for naturists. The island's remote nature ensures a peaceful experience, where the worries of the world seem a million miles away. It's the perfect place for beachcombing, enjoying picnics, and simply basking in the sun without a care.

For those looking to blend naturist activities with a bit of cultural exploration, British Columbia's numerous art festivals and local markets offer splendid opportunities. Many regional festivals welcome naturists, adding a celebratory atmosphere to your travels. Be it live music, performing arts, or artisan crafts, there's always something to experience and enjoy. These events provide a glimpse into the local culture and foster a sense of community among naturists.

Staying in British Columbia also means you can take advantage of the region's robust outdoor pursuits. Hiking, biking, and boating are just a few activities that can be enjoyed in the buff. Naturist-friendly trails are scattered throughout the province, with options catering to all levels of experience. Hiking through the dense forests and alpine meadows, you'll find that nature is at its most accessible and inviting when there are no barriers between you and the wild.

Don't overlook the importance of etiquette and local customs while exploring these naturist spots. Respecting others' comfort levels and adhering to signage is crucial. Most naturist areas are well-marked, but it's wise to stay informed about specific regulations. Remember, naturism in British Columbia is about fostering a respectful and relaxed community.

In addition to these stunning locations, the people you meet on your travels often add an enriching dimension to your experience. British Columbia's naturist community is known for its warmth and openness. It's easy to strike up conversations and build friendships, sharing stories and tips about the best spots or simply reveling in the shared experience of naturism.

So, why choose British Columbia for your naturist vacation? The answer lies in its unrivaled natural beauty, the diverse array of naturist spots, and the welcoming spirit of its people. Each destination here offers something special, whether it's the vibrant energy of Wreck Beach, the serene embrace of CottonTail Corner, or the mystical allure of Nakusp Hot Springs. In British Columbia, every sunset becomes a celebration, and every view feels like a masterpiece painted by nature. It's a place where you can be free, be yourself, and fully embrace the liberating joy of naturism.

Your journey through the breathtaking landscapes of British Columbia will undoubtedly leave a lasting impression. The memories you create and the connections you make will stay with you long after you depart. Embrace the natural beauty and the freedom that comes with it, and you'll understand why British Columbia stands out as a premier naturist destination.

Quebec Charms

Quebec, with its rich history and vibrant culture, is a hidden gem for naturists seeking unique and liberating experiences. This province, known for its stunning landscapes and welcoming locals, offers some of the best naturist destinations in North America. From tranquil lakeside retreats to lush forested areas, Quebec promises a mix of serenity and adventure that caters to both seasoned naturists and those new to the lifestyle.

Imagine being enveloped by nature as you stand on the shores of a pristine lake, the water's edge lapping gently at your feet. Quebec's naturist resorts often feature breathtaking scenery that feels almost untouched by time. These havens seamlessly blend the freedom of the outdoors with the comforts of modern amenities, making your stay as enjoyable as it is freeing. You'll find community and connection in these special places, where the motto "liberté, égalité, fraternité" truly comes to life.

One of the standout naturist spots in Quebec is the serene and lush La Pommerie, located in the Eastern Townships. This resort embodies the natural beauty and tranquility that the region is known for. The grounds are meticulously maintained, offering a variety of activities from leisurely nature walks to invigorating swims in the resort's clear waters. The atmosphere is relaxed, and the people you'll meet here are as warm as the sun on a summer day. At La Pommerie, naturists of all ages can find their perfect place to rejuvenate and connect with nature.

For those who crave a bit more adventure, Quebec also offers places like Domaine de l'Île Ronde. Situated on a private island, this naturist resort provides a unique blend of isolation and community. Accessible only by boat, the journey sets the tone for an experience that is as exciting as it is serene. Once on the island, you'll discover lush forests, sandy shores, and plenty of opportunities for water activities. It's a place where you can truly disconnect from the hustle of everyday life and immerse yourself in the soothing embrace of nature.

Navigating through Quebec's expressive cultural tapestry, you'll also find naturist-friendly events and festivals that highlight the province's joie de vivre. Events like the Festival Vivre nu provide a platform for naturists to celebrate their lifestyle openly and joyously. These gatherings are more than just social events; they are a testament to the inclusive and dynamic spirit of Quebec's naturist community.

Now, it's not all about resorts and events. A stunning naturist-friendly destination is Oka National Park. This park offers a clothing-optional beach, making it an ideal day trip for naturists exploring the Montreal area. With its expansive sandy beach and crystal-clear waters, Oka allows you to reconnect with nature and yourself. The park also features well-maintained trails that are perfect for hiking and discovering native wildlife. It's a versatile spot that beautifully captures Quebec's natural splendor.

Beyond the well-known resorts and parks, Quebec is dotted with hidden gems that are perfect for the more intrepid naturist. Small, community-run retreats offer a more intimate and secluded experience. These spots maintain a charm that's hard to find in more commercialized areas. They are often run by passionate individuals who genuinely love sharing the natural beauty of Quebec with others. The energy in these spaces is magnetic, drawing in those who seek a deeper, more personal naturist experience.

Adventures in Quebec aren't limited to summer months. Winter naturism is also embraced, offering a unique twist for those willing to venture into colder climates. Locations like the Nordic Station in Magog offer a blend of indoor and outdoor activities that continue year-round. Picture yourself warming up in a hot tub surrounded by snow-covered trees, the contrast between the cold air and steaming water invigorating your senses. Such experiences highlight Quebec's versatility as a naturist destination, providing opportunities for relaxation and adventure in every season.

Accommodations throughout Quebec vary widely, from rustic cabins to luxurious lodges. Many resorts offer all-inclusive packages that cover meals, activities, and accommodations, allowing you to focus entirely on your relaxation and enjoyment. Regardless of where you stay, expect warm hospitality and a welcoming atmosphere, true to the spirit of Quebec.

Quebec's naturist destinations also emphasize wellness and mindfulness. Many resorts offer yoga and meditation classes that encourage a deeper connection to oneself and the environment. These sessions often take place in serene settings, like a sun-dappled forest clearing or on a quiet lakeshore. Participating in these activities can rejuvenate your mind, body, and spirit, making your naturist vacation a holistic and enriching experience.

The food in Quebec is another essential part of the experience. Many naturist resorts feature local cuisine that celebrates the rich culinary heritage of the region. Think fresh, farm-to-table meals with ingredients sourced from local farmers and artisans. Outdoor dining is common, allowing you to enjoy your meals surrounded by the beauty of nature. The emphasis on quality and freshness in Quebec's cuisine adds another layer of pleasure to your stay.

Language barriers are rare, as most locals are bilingual or at least familiar with basic English. However, trying your hand at a few French phrases can add to the charm of your experience and is usually appreciated by the locals. Simple greetings like "Bonjour" and "Merci" can go a long way in making connections and enhancing your stay.

The blend of nature, culture, and community makes Quebec a must-visit for any naturist. Whether you're relaxing at a lakeside resort, participating in a naturist festival, or exploring a secluded beach, Quebec offers a wealth of experiences that are bound to leave a lasting impression. It's a place where you can truly be yourself, embraced by the welcoming spirit of the province.

In essence, Quebec charms with its diverse landscapes, rich culture, and inclusive naturist community. It's a destination that caters to the soul's desire for freedom and connection, a place where nature's beauty and human warmth create a setting like no other. Whether you're seeking tranquility, community, adventure, or renewal, Quebec stands ready to welcome you with open arms and boundless natural charm.

Mexico: Sun and Sand

Mexico, with its radiant sun, golden sands, and azure waters, is more than just a vacation spot—it's an invitation to rediscover your connection with nature in the most liberating way. The country's geographical diversity, from its serene Caribbean coastlines to its rugged Pacific shores, offers naturist travelers a plethora of paradisiacal retreats.

Nestled along the Riviera Maya, you'll find some of the most idyllic places for naturist experiences. Resorts like Hidden Beach Resort offer exclusive nude beach experiences where turquoise waves lap at your feet while you bask in the sun without a care. This all-inclusive, clothing-optional resort promises guests an atmosphere of freedom and relaxation, with high-end amenities and activities that cater specifically to naturists.

If you wander a bit further to the enchanting beach town of Tulum, you'll encounter stretches of pristine, palm-lined beaches. While Tulum isn't exclusively a naturist destination, its laid-back vibe and acceptance make it an accessible location for those who prefer to shed their layers. Many beaches here have pockets where you can find solitude and comfort in naturism.

On the Yucatan Peninsula, the blend of ancient Mayan culture and stunning natural landscapes provides an unforgettable backdrop to your naturist adventures. Playa del Carmen, often noted for its vibrant nightlife and bustling beach scene, also offers secluded spots for naturist activities. Amid the whispers of the Caribbean Sea, one can find discreet areas to experience the sun, sand, and sea au naturel.

Driving towards the Pacific, visit Zipolite—a beach town renowned for being the first and only legal public nudist beach in Mexico. Zipolite's motto, 'Relax and enjoy life,' encapsulates the spirit of this naturist haven. The beach hosts an annual nudist festival that draws visitors from around the globe, offering a chance to engage in yoga, beach sports, and social events with a distinctly naturist flavor.

In Baja California Sur, Cabo San Lucas and its sister city, San José del Cabo, provide more upscale naturist enclaves. Boutique resorts along the coast offer the perfect blend of luxury and liberating naturist experiences. Known for its spectacular diving, snorkeling, and whale watching, this region enriches your naturist holiday with adventure and awe.

While naturism in Mexico might not be as mainstream as in some European countries, there's a growing acceptance and fascination with the lifestyle. Many boutique hotels and resorts now market to naturist clientele, ensuring a burgeoning community of enthusiasts can enjoy these stunning locales.

The cultural richness of Mexico also comes into play when exploring its naturist potential. There's something magically hedonistic about a country with such deep-rooted traditions indulging in the freedom of naturism. These destinations provide a unique blend of cultural exploration and relaxation, making your trip educational and liberating.

While exploring the naturist beaches and resorts, don't miss out on the incredible local cuisine. There's nothing quite like savoring fresh ceviche or authentic tacos by the sea. The combination of flavors, aromas, and the bare essentials of nature creates a multisensory experience that's both invigorating and unforgettable.

Safety and community are paramount in these naturist havens. You'll find that the naturist locales in Mexico foster a friendly and welcoming environment. This camaraderie, combined with the scenic beauty, creates a perfect blend for solo travelers and groups alike. Whether it's a yoga retreat, a festive gathering, or just a tranquil afternoon by the shore, there's a space for every naturist to find their moment of zen.

As you prepare for your Mexican naturist journey, being mindful of the regional customs and guidelines will ensure a respectful and blissful experience. Naturism in Mexico offers an escape from the everyday, inviting you to connect deeply with the elements around you.

From the secluded beaches of Tulum to the spirited shores of Zipolite, Mexico's naturist destinations promise an extraordinary getaway. Here, the sun, sand, and spirit of freedom coalesce into an adventure that touches your soul and liberates your spirit. With warm hospitality, stunning natural beauty, and a growing naturist culture, Mexico stands out as a prime destination for those yearning to uncover the world—and themselves—in their most natural state.

Chapter 4:
Caribbean Paradises for Naturists

Picture the lush splendor of the Caribbean, where crystal-clear waters kiss powdery shores and the sun's embrace feels like a benevolent caress. This enchanting region is a haven for naturists seeking to merge with nature in its most pristine form. Amongst the gems are Jamaica's world-renowned nude beaches, offering the perfect blend of relaxation and adventure. The Bahamas, often whispered about for its hidden nude spots, provide secluded coves that invite tranquil, soul-soothing retreats. Then, the dual-named isle of St. Martin/St. Maarten, known for its uniquely European flair, presents a palette of naturist experiences ranging from lively beaches to quiet, untouched reserves. In these paradises, you'll discover more than just beautiful landscapes; it's an invitation to shed societal constraints, reconnect with the essence of being, and savor the liberation that comes from baring it all under the tropical sun.

Jamaica's Nude Beaches

Jamaica, a vibrant Caribbean island, is not only famed for its reggae beats and lush landscapes but also for its inviting nude beaches that offer a haven for naturists. The island's laid-back attitude, combined with its stunning natural beauty, makes it an ideal destination for those seeking liberation and connection with nature.

The most popular nude beach in Jamaica is Hedonism II, located in Negril. This resort offers an all-inclusive experience where clothing is optional and the atmosphere is inclusive and welcoming. Spread over 22 acres of beachfront property, Hedonism II provides a plethora of activities and amenities that cater to both seasoned naturists and curious newcomers.

The resort's private beach is divided into two sections: the prude beach and the nude beach. The prude beach allows for clothing, while the nude beach is strictly clothing-optional. This setup offers guests the freedom to ease into the naturist lifestyle at their own pace. Whether you choose to relax under the swaying palm trees, participate in water sports, or simply bask in the Jamaican sun, Hedonism II ensures a memorable and liberating experience.

If you're looking for a more secluded option, Little Beach in Negril is a fantastic choice. Nestled away from the bustling tourist areas, this beach provides a more tranquil and intimate setting. The soft, white sands and crystal-clear waters make it perfect for a day of unwinding and connecting with nature. Although it doesn't have the amenities of a resort, the natural beauty and peaceful atmosphere more than make up for it.

For those who desire a blend of resort luxury and the freedom of naturism, Couples Sans Souci in Ocho Rios offers an exquisite experience. This adults-only, all-inclusive resort features a private nude beach known as Sunset Beach. Here, naturists can enjoy a range of activities, from lounging by the pool to paddleboarding in the serene waters. The resort's lush gardens and elegant accommodations enhance the sense of escape and relaxation.

Beyond the beaches, Jamaica's warm and welcoming culture adds to the appeal of its naturist destinations. The island's residents are known for their friendliness and hospitality, making it easy for visitors to feel at home. Additionally, the country's legal stance on naturism is relatively relaxed, allowing for a more comfortable and stress-free experience.

While the popular resorts provide a structured environment for naturists, there are also plenty of opportunities to explore Jamaica's natural wonders. From the Blue Mountains to the majestic waterfalls, the island's diverse landscapes offer countless ways to connect with nature. Many visitors find that combining their beach experience with excursions into the island's interior provides a well-rounded and fulfilling trip.

For naturists seeking community and social connections, Jamaica hosts a variety of events and gatherings throughout the year. These events often feature yoga sessions, wellness workshops, and themed parties, creating opportunities to meet like-minded individuals and forge lasting friendships. Participating in these events can add an extra layer of enjoyment to your naturist vacation.

When planning your trip to Jamaica's nude beaches, it's essential to consider a few practical aspects. First, be mindful of the local customs and etiquette. While Jamaica is generally accepting of naturism, it's crucial to respect the boundaries of designated areas and adhere to the guidelines provided by resorts and beach authorities. Additionally, packing essentials such as sunscreen, beach towels, and light, breathable clothing can enhance your comfort and enjoyment.

Accommodation options in Jamaica are diverse, ranging from luxury resorts to quaint bed and breakfasts. For those who prefer budget-friendly options, there are also guesthouses and vacation rentals available. Planning your stay according to your preferences and budget can ensure a stress-free and enjoyable experience.

As you embark on your naturist adventure in Jamaica, remember that the essence of naturism lies in freedom, authenticity, and connection with nature. The island's nude beaches provide the perfect backdrop for embracing these principles, offering a sanctuary where you can let go of societal constraints and fully experience the beauty of the natural world.

Whether you're lounging on the pristine sands of Hedonism II, exploring the secluded charm of Little Beach, or indulging in the luxury of Couples Sans Souci, Jamaica's nude beaches promise an unforgettable and transformative experience. Each visit to this Caribbean paradise brings a new opportunity to reconnect with yourself and discover the true meaning of liberation.

So pack your bags, shed your inhibitions, and set off on an adventure to Jamaica's nude beaches—an unmatched blend of natural beauty, relaxation, and the timeless allure of naturism.

Hidden Gems in the Bahamas

Imagine stepping onto warm, white sand beaches, the ocean's turquoise waves lightly caressing your feet, and a gentle breeze wrapping around your bare skin. This image isn't just a daydream but a reality waiting for naturists in the Bahamas. Often overshadowed by its more famous Caribbean neighbors, the Bahamas offers tranquil, unspoiled spots perfect for those seeking freedom and connection with nature in its purest form.

The Bahamas consists of over 700 islands and cays, many of which remain largely unexplored by the average tourist. This archipelago offers an unparalleled opportunity to discover secluded beaches where you can lose your clothes amongst the splendor of sweeping coastal scenery and lush vegetation. One such treasure is Bird Cay. Located in the Berry Islands, Bird Cay is a private island that offers privacy, tranquility, and a sense of exclusivity that are hard to come by.

Bird Cay's beaches are pristine and rarely seen by outsiders, making it a delightful haven for naturists. Imagine snorkeling in crystal-clear waters teeming with vibrant marine life, every color more vivid against the unblemished white sand floor. Afterward, relax on the beach with not a soul in sight, the serenity only broken by the gentle rhythm of palm trees swaying in the breeze.

On Great Exuma, Tropic of Cancer Beach—also known as Pelican Beach—is a hidden gem inviting you to embrace nature in its raw form. Named for its location on the Tropic of Cancer, this beach boasts miles of soft, golden sand that seems to stretch into infinity. The remoteness of the place means fewer tourists, providing naturists with the space they crave to feel at one with nature. Picture basking under the tropical sun, soaking in both the charm of your surroundings and the liberating sensation of a naturist escape.

Another lesser-known spot is the secluded beach at the western tip of Stocking Island. Accessible only by boat, Stocking Island offers solitude and seclusion, with an array of idyllic nooks perfect for naturist activities. The western beach, in particular, has calm, shallow waters ideal for snorkeling or simply floating under the Caribbean sun. Imagine exploring hidden coves and tidal pools that invite you to shed your clothes and immerse yourself in nature's beauty without interruption.

The uninhabited island of Long Cay presents a pristine escape as well. Known for its exotic landscapes and untouched environment, Long Cay serves as a naturalist's paradise. Explore limestone cliffs, lush forests, and serene beaches, often without encountering another human being. Picture a picnic on warm sands, shaded by towering palms, with nothing to disturb the peace but the sound of the surf and the occasional chatter of tropical birds.

Let's not forget the serene Pink Sands Beach on Harbour Island. While Harbour Island is generally famous for its pastel-colored sands, the quiet northern end of Pink Sands Beach offers an experience that's less frequented by the casual vacationer. This part of the beach is perfect for naturists who wish to embrace the environment intimately. Imagine walking through sand that feels like powdered sugar under your feet and watching sunsets that turn the sky into a painter's palette—all while feeling completely free of barriers between you and Mother Earth.

Beyond the beaches, naturists can also explore the island's natural wonders and wildlife reserves. The Bahamas National Trust manages several parks and protected areas that offer a deeper connection to the flora and fauna of the islands. Horse Stall Beach on Mayaguana is an untouched natural landscape where birdwatching, hiking, and swimming can be enjoyed au naturel. The island's remoteness ensures privacy, allowing naturists to roam freely through mangroves and tropical gardens.

The underwater world of the Bahamas is equally mesmerizing. Andros Island, with its expansive barrier reef, offers naturist-friendly snorkeling and diving experiences. Dive sites near the island are often secluded, giving you the chance to explore underwater grottos and coral gardens unimpeded by crowds. Picture descending into crystalline waters, the world above melting away as you become one with the kaleidoscope of marine life around you.

In preparation for your Bahamian adventure, familiarizing yourself with local customs and courtesies is essential. Although there are no official naturist beaches in the Bahamas, the secluded and remote nature of these hidden gems offers naturists the freedom to enjoy their surroundings with a respect for privacy and discretion.

When planning your trip, consider staying in a naturist-friendly resort or renting a private villa to enhance your experience. The beauty of the Bahamas lies not only in its natural landscapes but also in the warmth and hospitality of its people. Make the most of your journey by respecting the local way of life and engaging with the community in a meaningful way.

Hidden gems in the Bahamas are more than just locations; they are experiences waiting to be discovered by those who seek the ultimate form of freedom and connection with nature. With its secluded beaches, calm waters, and diverse wildlife, the Bahamas offers an unparalleled canvas for naturists to paint their dreams. Imagine every worry washed away by the ocean's gentle tides, and every joy highlighted by the golden rays of the tropical sun.

In essence, the Bahamas is not just a destination but a state of mind, a sanctuary for those yearning to experience life unencumbered by the constraints of clothing and societal norms. It's a place where every turn offers a new corner of paradise to be discovered, and every wave whispers the promise of freedom. Ultimately, the hidden gems of the Bahamas aren't just about finding a place to go nude—they're about finding a place to truly feel alive.

Exploring St. Martin/St. Maarten

Cradled in the embrace of the azure Caribbean Sea, St. Martin/St. Maarten is a shining jewel for naturist travelers. This island, split between French and Dutch territories, offers a unique fusion of European refinement and Caribbean charm. With stunning beaches, vibrant markets, and a lively cultural scene, St. Martin/St. Maarten stands out as one of the premier destinations for those seeking a liberating nude vacation.

The French side (Saint Martin) is known for its relaxed attitude towards naturism, making it a preferred destination for nudists. Here, you can experience the joie de vivre while basking under the Caribbean sun without a care in the world. The Dutch side (Sint Maarten), though slightly more conservative, still offers pockets of leisure where clothing can be optional.

One of the prime naturist spots on the island is Orient Bay Beach on the French side. Often dubbed the "Saint-Tropez of the Caribbean," this beach provides the perfect setting for those who appreciate the freedom of naturism. The beach is divided; while part of it is family-friendly, another section is dedicated to naturist endeavors. The turquoise waters, pristine sands, and swaying palm trees create a paradisiacal backdrop for a carefree day under the sun.

From your first steps onto the soft sands of Orient Bay Beach, you can feel the island's welcoming nature. A leisurely stroll along the shore reveals vibrant beach bars, local eateries, and watersports facilities. Naturism here doesn't mean isolation; it means becoming part of a community that embraces body positivity and mutual respect.

For naturists who wish to explore more than just beaches, the island offers numerous other attractions. When you're ready for a break from the sun and sand, head into the heart of Marigot, the capital of the French side. Here, narrow streets lead to open-air markets, where you can lose yourself in the vibrant colors and aromatic smells of local produce, spices, and handmade crafts. The lazy rhythm of island life is infectious, setting the perfect stage for leisurely nude excursions.

Simpson Bay, on the Dutch side, is another must-visit locale. Though not exclusively naturist, many visitors find it comfortable to bare it all at quieter spots. Simpson Bay is famous for its bustling nightlife, and naturist-friendly resorts around the area offer the perfect blend of relaxation and entertainment.

For those who crave a bit of adventure, there are several boat trips that can take you around the island or to neighboring islets. Many of these excursions are endorsed by naturist-friendly operators, ensuring you can sunbathe and swim in the buff. Pinel Island is particularly popular, with secluded nude-friendly beaches and crystal-clear waters that are ideal for snorkeling.

Dining on the island is a culinary adventure, reflecting its French and Dutch influences. Many beachfront restaurants allow naturists to dine in the nude, especially on the French side. Picture yourself savoring fresh seafood, rich French cuisine, or Creole delights, all while watching a breathtaking Caribbean sunset. It's a romantic and liberating experience, etching unforgettable memories.

Accommodations range from luxurious resorts to more private villas and guesthouses. Several resorts not only allow but encourage naturism, providing amenities such as private nude beaches, nude pools, and clothing-optional restaurants and bars. These resorts focus on creating a comfortable and respectful environment where guests can enjoy their vacation exactly as they wish.

Beyond beaches and bustling markets, St. Martin/St. Maarten also invites naturists to delve into its natural beauty. Hiking trails like Loterie Farm offer the chance to explore the island's lush landscapes, often culminating in breathtaking views that can be enjoyed in your natural state. The trails are well-maintained and range in difficulty, making them suitable for both novice and experienced hikers.

In terms of cultural ambiance, St. Martin/St. Maarten is a melting pot. The island hosts numerous festivals throughout the year, celebrating everything from Carnival to local music and food. These events, while often clothed, contribute to the island's inclusive and festive spirit, enhancing your overall experience.

Traveling around the island is fairly straightforward. Renting a car is a popular choice and gives you the freedom to explore at your own pace. Most rental services are respectful of naturist travelers, given the island's tourism dynamics. Buses and taxis are readily available and reasonably priced, allowing easy access to various naturist spots.

Language is not a barrier here, with English being widely spoken alongside French and Dutch. This linguistic versatility adds to the island's appeal, making it easier for naturists from around the globe to feel at home. The locals are warm and welcoming, often going out of their way to share tips about hidden beaches or the best eateries.

Respect for local customs and the environment goes a long way in enhancing your naturist adventure. Engage with the community, sample the local cuisine, and always clean up after yourself on the beaches. These small gestures contribute to a sustainable and respectful naturist culture, ensuring such paradises continue to thrive.

In summary, St. Martin/St. Maarten offers a tapestry of experiences for naturists. Whether it's the allure of pristine beaches, the charm of local markets, or the adventure beckoning from hiking trails and boat trips, this island caters to all aspects of a naturist's dream vacation. So, allow the warm Caribbean breezes to caress your skin, feel the sand between your toes, and let St. Martin/St. Maarten liberate and inspire you in ways only a true naturist haven can.

Chapter 5:
South America's Naturist Getaways

South America offers an exhilarating blend of dazzling landscapes and secluded paradises for those seeking the freedom of naturist travel. Imagine yourself basking on the sun-soaked beaches of Brazil, where the rhythmic samba beats meet azure waves, or retreating to Argentina's hidden escapes, where lush forests cradle crystal-clear waters, creating the perfect backdrop for nature's embrace. Uruguay's understated charm will captivate your soul, with its peaceful retreats along the serene coastline. Whether it's the spirited ambiance of Brazil's coastal havens or the tranquil allure of Argentina and Uruguay, South America's naturist getaways promise an unforgettable journey of liberation and natural splendor.

Brazil's Coastal Havens

In South America's expansive canvas of naturist destinations, Brazil undoubtedly shines with its coastal splendors, drawing both seasoned naturists and curious newcomers. The country's extensive coastlines, stretching over 7,000 kilometers, are dotted with hidden beaches, enchanting towns, and luxurious resorts, all embracing the liberating spirit of naturism.

From the lively shores of Rio de Janeiro to the serene escapades in Florianópolis, Brazil offers an eclectic mix of naturist-friendly locales. Picture yourself basking under the sun at Praia do Abricó, Rio's only official naturist beach. Here, the juxtaposition of lush Atlantic

Rainforest and the rhythmic whisper of waves creates a haven where nature and nudity harmonize seamlessly.

Unwind in the picturesque setting of Tambaba Beach, located in Paraíba, northeastern Brazil. As one of the country's most beloved naturist beaches, Tambaba offers a unique policy – the mandatory clothing-free zone comes with a warm sense of freedom and acceptance. Tall cliffs encircle the sandy beach, offering not only privacy but also jaw-dropping views. The experience is serene, with the turquoise waters inviting you to leave behind daily stresses and embrace the simplicity of life.

Travel further down the coast to discover Pinho Beach in Santa Catarina, Brazil's first official naturist beach. Nestled in a secluded cove, Pinho Beach's clear waters and pristine sands provide the perfect backdrop for quiet reflection or a day of fun with like-minded individuals. You'll find that the community here is open and welcoming, eager to share stories and perhaps even some travel tips.

In addition to the more well-known destinations, Brazil conceals many smaller, lesser-known beaches that invite exploration and discovery. Praia da Galheta in Florianópolis, for instance, provides a less commercialized yet equally beautiful naturist experience. Accessed through a scenic trail that winds through lush vegetation, Galheta offers an unspoiled escape where the raw, untouched nature adds to the sense of liberation.

For those seeking an integrated resort experience where nudity extends beyond the beach, EcoParque da Mata in Bahia is an outstanding choice. This eco-retreat combines the tranquility of a naturist setting with a commitment to sustainability and environmental conservation. Far from the hustle and bustle, the resort allows you to reconnect with nature in a holistic, unhurried manner.

One cannot forget the charm of the small fishing village of Massarandupió, another Bahian jewel. This tranquil hideaway, with its expansive golden sands and warm Atlantic waters, promises a quintessentially Brazilian naturist experience. The beach here is renowned for its warm ambiance and spectacular sunsets, leaving an indelible mark on those who choose to visit.

But naturism in Brazil isn't limited to beaches alone. Resorts like Mirante do Paraíso offer comprehensive naturist experiences, with facilities designed to promote relaxation and well-being. Nestled amidst the lush Brazilian landscape, this retreat offers yoga sessions, meditation workshops, and therapeutic treatments, making it a sanctuary for both body and soul.

Brazil's mix of vivacious cities and tranquil retreats means there is something for every kind of naturist traveler. Whether seeking the buzz of urban beaches or the solace of hidden coves, Brazil's coastal havens are the perfect setting for naturist exploration. The locals' warm-hearted hospitality and the country's intrinsic natural beauty ensure that every moment spent in Brazil is both unique and unforgettable.

Argentina's Secluded Escapes

As you venture into South America's vast expanse, Argentina beckons with its diverse landscapes and the promise of secluded naturist experiences that resonate with both wild beauty and serene solitude. While Brazil's coastlines may initially steal the spotlight, Argentina offers more understated yet equally compelling destinations for naturist enthusiasts seeking peace and connection with nature.

Argentina's naturist escapes are not about crowded beaches or bustling resorts; they are intimate retreats nestled in nature's embrace. A unique allure awaits travelers who dare to explore beyond the conventional tourist paths. Imagine stepping into a world where the

Andes' rugged peaks provide a dramatic backdrop to softly meandering rivers and unspoiled forests. Here, amid Argentina's breathtaking scenery, naturist havens invite you to shed not just your clothes, but also the concerns of everyday life.

Begin your journey in the country's central regions, where small yet welcoming naturist clubs and farms offer an idyllic retreat. These places are more than just escapes; they are communities where like-minded individuals gather to celebrate the freedom and simplicity that naturism brings. Clubs such as Yatan Rumi near Córdoba offer rustic accommodations and are nestled in landscapes that feel both ancient and untouched. It is here that one can truly disconnect, wandering through sprawling fields dotted with wildflowers, or dipping into cool, clear streams that twist through verdant valleys.

Travel further south and you'll find Patagonia's untamed beauty—a region as captivating as its name suggests. The sheer diversity of Patagonia's geography, from arid steppes to lush forests and icy glaciers, creates a multitude of secluded spots perfect for naturist adventures. Hidden in this expanse are remote cabins and camping spots where the sense of isolation is profound, yet deeply comforting. Here, under the immense canvas of the Patagonian sky, you can experience naturism in its most elemental form. Bathing in a secluded waterfall or hiking a forest trail in the buff, you'll find that removing the barriers between yourself and nature fosters a powerful sense of belonging and tranquility.

In the northeast, the province of Misiones is home to lush rainforests and the awe-inspiring Iguazu Falls. While not traditionally associated with naturism, hidden gems in this region cater to those in the know. Private eco-lodges and remote areas within protected parks offer naturist-friendly policies. Imagine standing on a balcony overlooking the thunderous falls, feeling the mist against your bare skin, and knowing that you are mere steps away from tranquil forest trails where you can wander freely.

Mar del Plata, often referred to as Argentina's "Happy City," may be better known for its bustling beaches and nightlife, but some less-traveled paths lead to quieter, more private locations. Naturist-friendly areas like El Edén offer sanctuary amidst sand dunes and sheltered coves. In these retreats, the rhythm of the waves and the call of seabirds form the soundtrack to your days, making for a rejuvenating escape from the everyday retreat.

Another gem lies in the province of Entre Ríos. Nestled among the region's gentle hills and expansive rivers, you will find La Serena Naturist Complex. This retreat prides itself on blending comfort with a profound respect for nature. Imagine immersing yourself in natural thermal pools, surrounded by the serenity of native woodlands. Whether it's a quiet walk through shaded trails or yoga practice on a sun-drenched terrace, the ethos here is one of peace and reconnection.

Why do naturists cherish such places? The answer lies in the intrinsic human desire to reconnect—both with ourselves and with the environment around us. Naturist spots in Argentina offer more than just serene settings; they provide a sense of community and a shared understanding of the precious liberation that comes with shedding societal constraints. There's something unifying about meeting others who embrace the same philosophies, fostering a sense of camaraderie and mutual respect.

While Buenos Aires might seem an unusual starting point for a naturist journey, the city acts as a convenient gateway. From Buenos Aires, easy flights and scenic drives connect you to Argentina's naturist spots. After sampling the vibrant culture, cuisine, and history of the cosmopolitan capital, the transition to the quietude of Argentina's secluded naturist escapes feels like a poetic contrast.

Choosing Argentina for a naturist adventure also means enjoying a country rich in culture and history. The locals' warm hospitality, the mouth-watering cuisine, and the country's storied past enrich the entire experience. Whether engaging in conversations over a traditional Asado (barbecue) or learning about the indigenous cultures, every moment adds to the depth of your journey.

Practical considerations for aspiring naturist travelers to Argentina are relatively straightforward. Unlike more densely populated destinations, these secluded spots offer tranquility without the need for extensive planning or reservations. However, understanding local customs and respecting the community's norms is crucial. Small gestures, like learning a few Spanish phrases or being mindful of environmental conservation practices, can go a long way in ensuring a harmonious stay.

As you ponder your next naturist escape, let Argentina's secluded sanctuaries call out to you. Picture yourself in the embrace of uncharted wilderness, where every sunrise and sunset paints the sky with hues that invite contemplation and peace. Each day spent soaking in the freedom of naturism deepens your appreciation for the natural world and your place within it.

Argentina's insulated retreats stand as testament to the timeless appeal of solitude and nature. They remind us that some of the best journeys involve not just discovering new places, but also rediscovering ourselves. Here, in the heart of South America's diverse landscapes, the spirit of naturism thrives, offering unparalleled freedom and connections that transcend the ordinary. Let this be your invitation to explore, transform, and truly embrace the liberating beauty of Argentina's secluded escapes.

Naturist Retreats in Uruguay

South America is a tapestry of vibrant cultures, lush landscapes, and stunning coastlines. Nestled within this remarkable continent, Uruguay emerges as a serene haven for naturists seeking a unique blend of tranquility and vitality. The nation's relaxed attitude towards naturism and its commitment to maintaining pristine natural environments make it an irresistible destination for those wanting to shed their clothes and the chaos of everyday life.

Uruguay, known for its charming colonial towns and progressive social policies, offers a tantalizing array of naturist retreats that promise freedom and rejuvenation. Montevideo, the capital city, is often the starting point for many visitors. Its coastal stretches, particularly Playa Chihuahua, provide the perfect introduction to the country's naturist gateways.

Imagine walking barefoot on Playa Chihuahua, the sand warm and comforting beneath your feet. Here, the Atlantic Ocean extends into an endless horizon, its waves whispering tales of ancient mariners. This official naturist beach is just a short drive from Punta del Este, the glamorous beach resort famous for its vibrant nightlife and luxurious accommodations. Yet, Playa Chihuahua is a stark contrast to the bustling city life, offering a peaceful escape where visitors can sunbathe and swim in the nude.

Not far from Punta del Este, the secluded cove of Playa La Sirena invites naturist enthusiasts into its intimate embrace. This hidden gem is renowned for its golden sands and crystal-clear waters, ideal for those seeking solace in nature's beauty. The gentle rustling of leaves and the melodic songs of native birds heighten the sense of privacy and harmony here. Though not officially designated as a naturist beach, Playa La Sirena has garnered a reputation for being welcoming to the nudist community.

The breathtaking coastal town of Rocha also beckons to naturist travelers. Known for its untamed beaches and protected parks, Rocha is a paradise for naturalists and naturists alike. Within this region, Cabo Polonio stands out—accessible only by four-wheel drive vehicles or on foot, this remote village is a utopia of rustic charm and natural beauty. No electricity, no paved roads; just the sound of the ocean, the scent of the sea, and the freedom to exist as one with the surroundings. Visiting Cabo Polonio is not just a trip; it is an invitation to disconnect profoundly from the modern world. Spend a day lounging on the beach, or hike up to the iconic lighthouse for panoramic views that capture the essence of Uruguay's raw splendor.

While the beaches are undeniably alluring, Uruguay offers more than just coastal escapes. The country hosts several naturist resorts that cater to visitors throughout the year. One such retreat is Refugio Naturista El Refugio, located in the scenic countryside near Montevideo. El Refugio provides a holistic naturist experience, combining the tranquility of rural landscapes with amenities designed to enhance relaxation and social interaction. Whether lounging by the pool or enjoying a communal meal, guests are encouraged to embrace the naturist lifestyle in a safe and supportive community.

In addition to El Refugio, Talar Naturist Club, situated near the charming town of Piriápolis, offers another enticing option. This club focuses on creating a family-friendly environment where visitors can enjoy outdoor activities such as hiking, swimming, and barbecuing in the nude. The club's motto, "nude in harmony with nature," reflects its commitment to promoting a respectful and environmentally conscious naturist experience.

Uruguay's warm climate and hospitality make it an ideal destination for naturist travelers seeking both solitude and community. As you meander through local markets, sampling artisanal cheeses and wines, or converse with friendly locals who take pride in their country's natural beauty, you will find that the leisurely pace of life here complements the naturist philosophy perfectly.

Naturism in Uruguay is not just about physical nudity; it's an immersive journey into a culture that values simplicity, respect, and connectivity with nature. Whether you're a seasoned naturist or a newcomer to the lifestyle, Uruguay has something to offer. Its unspoiled beaches, welcoming resorts, and serene landscapes ensure that every traveler leaves with a renewed sense of freedom and appreciation for the natural world.

While Uruguay's naturist spots are indeed captivating, remember to engage responsibly with local customs and the environment. Uruguayans take great pride in their country's ecological heritage, so practicing "leave no trace" principles and supporting local businesses are just as important as enjoying the freedom of nudity. By doing so, you help preserve these idyllic retreats for future generations of naturist enthusiasts.

In conclusion, Uruguay's naturist retreats offer a harmonious blend of natural beauty and cultural richness. From the windswept sands of Playa Chihuahua to the secluded charm of Cabo Polonio, this diminutive nation punches above its weight in delivering unforgettable naturist experiences. Each beach, each resort, and every sunset witnessed in your most natural state will etch memories of liberation, serenity, and unity with nature into your soul. So, pack light, leave your worries behind, and let Uruguay's naturist retreats redefine your idea of paradise.

Chapter 6:
Western Europe's Naturist Capitals

Western Europe stands as a beacon for naturists, offering some of the most iconic and liberating destinations. France, the birthplace of modern naturism, continues to enchant with the sun-soaked Cap d'Agde and the ruggedly beautiful nude beaches of Corsica. Spain's warm embrace calls from the golden sands of Costa del Sol to the exotic allure of the Canary Islands. Meanwhile, the Netherlands, with its liberal and free-spirited culture, offers serene naturist retreats harmonizing seamlessly with its picturesque landscapes. Each of these regions provides a unique tapestry of experiences, where the joy of being nude in nature meets rich cultural histories, offering the perfect escape for any naturist traveler dreaming of an idyllic European adventure.

France: The Birthplace of Modern Naturism

France stands as a beacon for naturists worldwide, carrying the proud title of the birthplace of modern naturism. The country first embraced the liberating lifestyle in the early 20th century, turning it into not just a travel option, but a rich cultural tradition. From the renowned beaches of Cap d'Agde to less crowded sanctuaries, France offers an enticing variety of destinations for those seeking harmony with nature. Envisage sun-kissed afternoons on golden sands and evenings spent in rustic naturist communities, where the ethos of acceptance and freedom permeates every interaction. France's dedication to naturism is palpable, making it a must-visit for anyone looking to explore a true haven of body-positive experiences enveloped in history, romance, and scenic landscapes.

Cap d'Agde: Naturist Village is a vibrant and legendary destination, often referred to as the "Naked City." Nestled in the South of France, this unique enclave is nestled along the Mediterranean coastline. It's a place where the naturist lifestyle isn't just accepted, it's celebrated. This village offers a sanctuary of freedom, allowing visitors to shed their clothes and embrace the authenticity of being human. With its sprawling beaches, lively atmosphere, and dedicated amenities, Cap d'Agde is truly a naturist's dream come true.

Walking through Cap d'Agde, you'll notice the harmonious coexistence of its residents and visitors. Here, naturism is a way of life, deeply ingrained in the culture and ethos of the village. From the moment you step into this enclave, clothes become an afterthought. Everyone, regardless of age or body type, confidently strolls the streets, enjoys cafés, shops, and even attends wellness centers without a stitch of clothing. There is an overwhelming sense of acceptance and camaraderie that envelops you, making you feel at ease and at home.

The centerpiece of Cap d'Agde's allure is its magnificent naturist beach. Stretching for miles, this sandy paradise invites you to bask in the Mediterranean sun without the constraints of swimwear. The beach is well-maintained, with azure waters that offer a refreshing escape from the heat. Water sports enthusiasts will find plenty to do, from windsurfing to paddleboarding. For those seeking relaxation, the gentle waves and soft sands provide the perfect backdrop for tranquility. Families, couples, and solo travelers mingle here, all united by the shared joy of naturism.

Accommodations in Cap d'Agde cater specifically to the naturist lifestyle. From luxurious beachfront hotels to cozy apartments and campsites, this village offers something for every budget and preference. Staying at naturist-friendly lodgings enhances the experience, allowing guests to remain in their natural state throughout their stay. Many properties feature amenities like nude pools, sauna facilities, and direct beach access, creating a seamless transition between relaxation and recreation.

The village itself is a hub of activity, teeming with shops, restaurants, and markets. Each establishment embraces the naturist ethos, allowing customers to shop and dine in the nude. Iconic spots include outdoor eateries serving fresh Mediterranean cuisine and quaint boutiques offering unique souvenirs. Walking through the open-air markets, you'll find local artisans displaying handcrafted goods, fresh produce, and regional delicacies. The smells, sounds, and sights of Cap d'Agde's markets are not to be missed.

During the evenings, Cap d'Agde comes alive with a different kind of energy. The nightlife here is vibrant and varied, with bars, clubs, and lounges offering an array of entertainment options. Music, dancing, and socializing continue well into the night, providing a lively contrast to the daytime serenity of the beaches. Whether you're enjoying a quiet cocktail at a beachfront bar or dancing the night away at one of the village's renowned nightclubs, the communal spirit of Cap d'Agde is ever-present.

For those interested in wellness and self-care, Cap d'Agde offers several opportunities to rejuvenate both body and mind. Wellness centers and spas provide services ranging from massages to yoga classes, all conducted in the nude. Engaging in these activities while surrounded by like-minded individuals can be deeply grounding, enhancing the sense of liberation and self-acceptance that defines naturism. Many visitors find that the combination of sun, sea, and wellness practices make for a highly restorative experience.

Exploring beyond the village limits, you'll find the picturesque landscapes of the Languedoc-Roussillon region waiting to be discovered. Day trips to nearby vineyards and historic towns add a cultural layer to your naturist holiday. The region's rich history and natural beauty offer a perfect counterbalance to the village's vibrant energy. Whether you're sampling local wines, exploring medieval architecture, or hiking through scenic trails, the possibilities for adventure are endless.

One of the remarkable aspects of Cap d'Agde is its inclusivity. The village welcomes naturists from all walks of life, fostering a diverse community that spans cultures and nationalities. This melting pot of perspectives and experiences creates a dynamic environment where everyone feels valued and accepted. It's not uncommon to make lifelong friends here, as the shared experience of naturism often leads to deep and meaningful connections.

When planning your trip to Cap d'Agde, it's important to immerse yourself in the local ethos. Respect for others and a non-judgmental attitude are fundamental. Observing proper naturist etiquette, such as carrying a towel to sit on in public places and understanding the local customs, enhances your experience and shows respect for the community. Preparation and understanding will enrich your time in this extraordinary village.

Safety and comfort are also central tenets of Cap d'Agde's community. The village is designed with naturist-friendly facilities, including dedicated security and medical services. Public spaces are clean and well-maintained, ensuring a pleasant environment for all. The sense of safety and acceptance here allows visitors to fully embrace their naturist journey without hesitation.

Visiting Cap d'Agde is more than just a vacation; it's an immersion into a lifestyle that celebrates freedom and authenticity. Whether you're a seasoned naturist or someone curious about this liberating way of life, the village offers an unparalleled experience. Relish in the sun-drenched days on the beach, the convivial evenings filled with laughter and music, and the profound sense of community that makes this destination truly unique. Cap d'Agde stands out not only as a naturist haven but as a testament to the joys of living life unapologetically and in harmony with oneself and others.

Corsica's Nude Beaches stand out as some of the most enticing in Europe, offering a perfect blend of natural beauty and a liberating atmosphere. Tucked away in the Mediterranean, Corsica boasts a collection of pristine beaches where naturism is not just permitted but celebrated. This French island, known for its rugged mountains and crystal-clear waters, provides an inviting haven for those eager to shed their clothes and connect with nature.

For many, discovering Corsica's nude beaches starts with the renowned *Plage de Saleccia*. This beach's long stretch of white sand and turquoise waters make it an ideal spot for naturists. While its remote location—accessible primarily by boat or a four-wheel-drive vehicle—may seem challenging, this very remoteness ensures a peaceful, crowd-free experience. The untouched beauty of Saleccia allows visitors to immerse themselves fully, feeling the warm sand underfoot and the sun on their skin.

Another notable destination is *Plage de Rondinara*, nestled in a horseshoe-shaped bay. The shallow, calm waters are perfect for swimming, making it a family-friendly option within the naturist community. Despite its popularity, Rondinara manages to maintain its tranquility, partly due to the spacious beach area that offers plenty of room for everyone. Whether you're laying out to tan or taking a dip in the inviting sea, the serenity of Rondinara is unmatched.

For those who crave a bit more seclusion, *Plage de Tahiti* near Porto-Vecchio is a hidden gem. This beach, surrounded by lush vegetation, provides an intimate and private setting for naturists. It's the kind of place where you can effortlessly let go of worldly worries and simply embrace the beauty around you. The water here is remarkably clear, inviting you to wade out and explore the vibrant marine life just beneath the surface.

Corsica's nude beaches aren't just limited to serene spots—they also include more lively and social areas like *Plage de Piantarella*. Located near Bonifacio, this beach is a favorite among water sports enthusiasts. Windsurfing and kitesurfing are common activities, adding a dash of excitement to the naturist experience. After an exhilarating day on the water, lounging on the sandy shores with fellow naturists can be both relaxing and communal, fostering a sense of shared freedom.

Exploring Corsica's coast wouldn't be complete without a visit to *Plage de Santa Giulia*. This beach's calm, shallow lagoon is ideal for swimming and snorkeling. With its fine sand and gentle slopes, Santa Giulia is perfect for families wanting a safe, beautiful environment to enjoy naturism together. The surrounding pine trees offer shaded spots, perfect for picnics and lazy afternoons with loved ones.

Another iconic beach is *Plage de Palombaggia*, often featured in travel magazines for its stunning scenery. Known for its sweeping coastline and transparent waters, Palombaggia attracts naturists who appreciate both natural beauty and convenience, given its relatively easy accessibility. It's a place where the essence of Corsica—wild and welcoming—can be felt in every breeze and wave. Exploring its rocky outcrops and coves can feel like a personal adventure, with each turn revealing another breathtaking view.

What sets Corsica's nude beaches apart isn't just their beauty but also the island's commitment to naturist principles. The local culture is open and accepting, making it easy for naturists to feel comfortable and welcome. There's a strong sense of community here, where the shared experience of naturism fosters connections between visitors. This camaraderie helps newcomers ease into the naturist lifestyle, surrounded by supportive and like-minded individuals.

Moreover, the island's amenities cater well to nudists, with several naturist campsites and resorts available. These establishments not only offer beachfront access but also provide facilities and activities aligned with naturist philosophies. Staying at a naturist resort, such as *Village Naturiste de Bagheera*, means immersing yourself in a holistic nudist experience, where every aspect of your stay is thoughtfully designed to honor the naturist way of life.

One can't help but feel a sense of liberation on Corsica's nude beaches. It's a place where societal norms dissolve, allowing you to reconnect with your natural state. The sense of freedom here is palpable, transforming a simple beach day into a profound experience of self-acceptance and unity with the environment. Whether you're indulging in the solitude of an isolated cove or mingling with fellow naturists at a popular spot, Corsica offers a naturist experience like no other.

As you wander these stunning shores, the harmony between the natural world and the naturist lifestyle becomes evident. Corsica's landscape—diverse and untouched—mirrors the raw authenticity that naturism seeks to embrace. Every beach, from the secluded to the communal, offers a unique window into the island's soul, creating memorable experiences that linger long after the journey ends.

Spain: Nude Under the Sun

Spain is a naturist's dream with its extensive coastline and sun-soaked landscapes inviting you to shed your clothes and indulge in the pure pleasure of feeling the sun and breeze all over your body. From the vibrant beaches of the Costa del Sol to the serene, hidden bays of the Canary Islands, Spain offers a varied palette of experiences for the naturist traveler. Whether you are a first-timer or a seasoned naturist, Spain's welcoming and open attitude towards nudism ensures a liberating and unforgettable adventure. Wander freely and revel in the sheer joy of naturism in this sun-drenched paradise.

Costa del Sol conjures images of vibrant Spanish culture, sun-kissed beaches, and a liberating atmosphere that makes it a prime destination for naturist travel. Stretching along the southern coast of Spain, this region is blessed with a temperate climate, stunning coastlines, and a rich cultural heritage that makes it perfect for those seeking to shed their inhibitions along with their clothes.

One of the most alluring aspects of Costa del Sol is its abundance of beautiful sandy beaches. The Mediterranean Sea laps gently along the shore, creating ideal conditions for sunbathing and swimming. Playa Artola, also known as Cabopino Beach, stands out as a must-visit spot. This wide expanse of fine golden sand is backed by natural dunes and offers designated naturist areas where one can bask in the sun's warmth without a care.

The region is both relaxed and welcoming, and naturists will find themselves at ease amidst the friendly locals and fellow travelers. The sociable ambiance allows for easy conversation and the formation of new friendships, often without the barriers that come with more conventional travel experiences. However, it's important to note that, like all naturist destinations, Costa del Sol has particular zones where nudity is permitted and respected.

Beyond the alluring beaches, the Costa del Sol offers plenty of cultural and recreational activities. Málaga, the capital of the Costa del Sol, is a treasure trove of historical and artistic attractions. The birthplace of Pablo Picasso, this city offers art lovers an array of museums, including the prestigious Picasso Museum. Wandering through its narrow streets, you'll stumble upon centuries-old architecture that tells tales of its Moorish past.

For those who wish to combine their love for naturism with a bit of adventure, there's no shortage of outdoor activities. Hiking enthusiasts can explore the picturesque trails of the Sierra de Mijas, offering panoramic views of the coastline and the lush Andalusian countryside. These excursions provide a perfect blend of liberation and nature, making it a holistic experience.

The culinary scene along the Costa del Sol is another reason to fall in love with the region. Indulging in Spanish tapas, fresh seafood, and local wines becomes a celebration of the senses. Many naturist-friendly establishments offer al fresco dining, allowing you to continue enjoying the natural atmosphere. From beachside chiringuitos to sophisticated urban dining, there's something to satisfy every palate.

The cultural vibrancy of the area also means that visitors can partake in various local festivals and events. The lively fairs, live music performances, and traditional flamenco shows are experiences not to be missed. Each fiesta is a burst of colors, sounds, and emotions that only enrich the liberating feeling of being in one of the world's best naturist destinations.

Accommodations in Costa del Sol cater to every type of traveler and range from luxurious resorts to charming beachside bungalows. Various naturist-friendly accommodations ensure that you can enjoy your stay without compromising on comfort or convenience. Many establishments come complete with pools, wellness centers, and other amenities that align perfectly with the naturist ethos of relaxation and well-being.

It's vital to be aware of local customs and regulations concerning naturism to ensure a respectful and enjoyable experience for everyone. Although the region is quite open-minded, it's still important to practice common courtesies, such as covering up in non-naturist zones and following posted guidelines at beaches and resorts.

In essence, Costa del Sol embodies the perfect combination of natural beauty, welcoming communities, and enriching activities that make it an unrivaled destination for naturist travels. Whether you are looking to unwind on breathtaking beaches, explore cultural landmarks, or engage in outdoor adventures, this Spanish haven provides an experience that is as freeing as it is unforgettable.

So, embrace the warmth, feel the sun on your skin, and let the rhythm of the Mediterranean guide your explorations. Costa del Sol isn't just a destination; it's a celebration of life in its most natural and beautiful form.

Canary Islands - a place where the azure waters of the Atlantic meet the liberated spirit of naturism. Located off the northwest coast of Africa, this magnificent archipelago consists of seven islands, each with its own unique charm. The Canary Islands are a sanctuary for those seeking an idyllic combination of stunning landscapes, warm climate, and a welcoming atmosphere for naturists. Here, you'll find some of the most pristine nude beaches, world-class resorts, and vibrant local culture that makes every visit an unforgettable adventure.

One of the crown jewels of the Canary Islands is *Fuerteventura*. Known for its expansive sandy beaches and crystalline waters, Fuerteventura is a paradise for naturists. One of the most popular spots is *Sotavento Beach*, a vast expanse of golden sand surrounded by turquoise lagoons. Whether you're lounging by the waters or taking a refreshing dip, Sotavento offers a perfect blend of relaxation and natural beauty. It's not just the beach that draws visitors; the island's laid-back vibe and ample sunshine make it a year-round destination.

Lanzarote, another awe-inspiring island in the Canaries, offers a dramatic landscape carved by volcanic activity. The island's unique black sand beaches and natural formations make it a truly remarkable place to explore. For naturists, *Charco del Palo* is a dream come true. This coastal village has embraced naturism since the early 1970s, providing a safe and comfortable environment for visitors. Charco del Palo is well-developed, featuring naturist-friendly accommodations, restaurants, and even grocery stores. Walking through its quiet streets and along its rugged coastline, you'll quickly feel at ease with the island's liberating ethos.

A visit to the Canaries wouldn't be complete without experiencing *Tenerife*, the largest of the islands. Tenerife is famous for its diverse landscapes, from lush forests and mountainous regions to its stunning beaches. *Playa de la Tejita* stands out as a naturist haven, located near the majestic Montaña Roja (Red Mountain). This secluded beach provides a peaceful retreat where you can bask in the sun and feel free from the constraints of clothing. Beyond the beach, Tenerife offers a rich cultural experience, with vibrant local markets, traditional fiestas, and exquisite cuisine. Don't miss a chance to try the local wines, crafted from grapes grown in the volcanic soil.

Gran Canaria is an island that perfectly blends natural beauty with lively social scenes. It's well-known among naturists for *Maspalomas* and its famous dunes. Spanning over 400 hectares, the dunes offer a unique and enchanting landscape that feels almost otherworldly. Naturists often gather at the far end of the beach, where the dunes meet the Atlantic, creating a perfect balance between seclusion and community. The nearby Yumbo Center in Playa del Inglés provides an engaging nightlife and entertainment scene, allowing you to experience both tranquility and excitement during your stay.

La Palma, known as "La Isla Bonita," is one of the quieter islands, ideal for those seeking solitude and the untouched beauty of nature. The island boasts numerous hidden coves and beaches where naturism is embraced. *Playa de las Monjas* is one such gem, offering a serene environment away from the bustling tourist spots. The island's rich biodiversity, lush forests, and volcanic landscapes also provide ample opportunities for hiking and exploring, making it a perfect destination for eco-conscious naturists.

For those wanting to experience a different side of the Canary Islands, *El Hierro* and *La Gomera* provide a more off-the-beaten-path adventure. These lesser-known islands offer rugged terrains, isolated beaches, and a slower pace of life. While naturist facilities are less developed here, the opportunity to connect deeply with unspoiled nature is unrivaled. The natural beauty of these islands is breathtaking, and their remote beaches provide the ultimate escape from the bustle of everyday life.

The Canary Islands not only offer stunning naturist beaches but also a sense of cultural richness and hospitality that defines the region. The islands are home to several traditional villages and towns where you can immerse yourself in the local way of life. Festivals, music, and dance are integral parts of Canarian culture. Visiting during one of the many local fiestas — such as Carnival or Los Indianos — you can witness firsthand the islands' vibrant traditions. These events often feature performances, parades, and celebrations that welcome everyone, including naturists.

When planning your visit, consider the best time to travel. The Canary Islands benefit from a subtropical climate, with mild temperatures year-round, making it an ideal destination at any time. However, the months of May through October are particularly favorable for enjoying the beaches and outdoor activities. During these months, the ocean is warmer, and the days are longer, giving you more time to soak in the sun and explore the natural beauty of the islands.

Getting around the Canary Islands can be an adventure in itself. While each island has its own airport, inter-island ferries offer a scenic mode of travel and allow you to experience the diverse character of each island. Rental cars are readily available and provide the flexibility to discover secluded beaches and hidden spots at your own pace.

Public transportation, such as buses, is also available and can be a convenient way to navigate the more populated islands like Tenerife and Gran Canaria.

Accommodations in the Canary Islands cater to all types of travelers, from luxury resorts to more rustic, eco-friendly lodgings. Many resorts and hotels in naturist-friendly areas offer specific amenities and services for naturists, ensuring comfort and ease throughout your stay. If you prefer a more immersive experience, consider staying in a traditional Canarian finca (farmhouse) or a coastal apartment, many of which welcome naturist guests. These options often provide a more intimate connection with the local landscape and culture.

As you embark on your naturist journey to the Canary Islands, keep in mind the importance of respect and etiquette. Naturism is widely accepted in designated areas and beaches, but it's always essential to be mindful of local customs and regulations. Practicing discretion and courtesy helps in maintaining the harmonious relationship between naturists and the local communities.

In summary, the Canary Islands offer a vibrant and varied naturist experience, combining breathtaking natural landscapes, warm hospitality, and a rich cultural heritage. Whether you're relaxing on the sun-soaked beaches of Fuerteventura, exploring the volcanic wonders of Lanzarote, or savoring the tranquil beauty of La Palma, each island promises a unique blend of adventure and serenity. The Canaries stand as a testament to the true spirit of naturism, where freedom, nature, and culture converge to create an unparalleled paradise.

The Netherlands: Liberal and Free

The Netherlands stands out as a pinnacle of liberal values, making it a fantastic destination for those interested in naturism. With a reputation for being open-minded and progressive, the Netherlands offers an environment where naturism is not just accepted but embraced with enthusiasm. From the bustling cityscapes of Amsterdam to the tranquil countryside, naturists will find a range of options to suit every preference.

A key part of the Dutch lifestyle is the concept of "gezelligheid," which loosely translates to coziness or conviviality. This sense of warmth and togetherness is palpable in naturist communities throughout the country. Whether lounging on a beach or mingling at a naturist resort, visitors will feel welcomed and at ease.

Nudity is more than tolerated; it's an expression of freedom and equality. Public nudity is allowed in designated areas, and the Dutch are known for their tolerant and non-judgmental attitudes. This makes it easier for newcomers to naturism to relax and fully enjoy the experience without feeling self-conscious.

Naturist beaches, known as "naaktstrand" in Dutch, are plentiful. One of the most famous is Zandvoort Beach, located just a short trip from Amsterdam. Known for its fine sand and clear waters, this beach attracts a diverse crowd, from dedicated naturists to curious first-timers. The unobtrusive lifeguards and well-maintained facilities contribute to a sense of safety and comfort.

Venturing further afield, you'll discover the Wadden Islands, a captivating archipelago in the northern Netherlands. Schiermonnikoog, the smallest of these islands, is largely a national park and offers extensive, secluded beaches perfect for naturist activities. The island's unspoiled nature and serene atmosphere make it an ideal retreat for those looking to disconnect from the hustle and bustle.

Moreover, Dutch naturist resorts are designed to cater to various tastes and lifestyles. Places like Naturistenpark Flevo-Natuur in Almere showcase the country's laid-back approach to naturist living. The park features extensive facilities, including swimming pools, saunas, and sports facilities, making it a comprehensive destination for naturist enthusiasts. Visitors often speak highly of the community spirit and friendly atmosphere, which are hallmarks of Dutch naturist culture.

It's not just coastal areas and designated resorts that welcome naturists. Many rural areas have trails and natural preserves where naturism is accepted. Walking through these picturesque landscapes in the nude can be a liberating experience, bringing a deeper connection with nature that textiled experiences simply can't match.

Dutch naturist clubs and associations play an active role in promoting naturism and educating the public. These organizations host events, workshops, and gatherings that create a sense of community and support. For instance, the Dutch Naturist Federation (NFN) is a significant body that advocates for naturist rights and organizes various activities across the country. Joining such a group can provide valuable insights and enhance your naturist experience in the Netherlands.

Regular social events like nude bowling, yoga classes, and boating trips also punctuate the Dutch naturist calendar. These activities offer a fun and engaging way to meet like-minded individuals while enjoying the freedom of a naturist lifestyle. The relaxed and friendly nature of these gatherings ensures that everyone, from seasoned naturists to beginners, can participate comfortably.

For those interested in combining naturism with cultural exploration, the Netherlands offers an unparalleled mix of activities. Museums, historical sites, and vibrant cities like Amsterdam and Rotterdam are easily accessible. You can immerse yourself in Dutch art, history, and culture during the day and retreat to a naturist-friendly environment by evening, blending the best of both worlds seamlessly.

Even in urban settings, the Netherlands maintains its liberal stance. While public nudity isn't allowed throughout city centers, certain urban beaches and parks do permit it. So, if you find yourself drawn to the dynamic energy of the city but still want a naturist experience, options such as Amsterdam's Amsterdamse Bos—to the south of the city—provide a refreshing escape.

The culinary scene in the Netherlands also reflects its liberal ethos. Naturist resorts and communities often feature communal dining experiences that encourage social interaction and sharing. Farm-to-table concepts are popular, emphasizing fresh, locally sourced ingredients. Enjoying a meal in the nude can be an unexpectedly delightful experience, further enhancing the sense of freedom that naturism brings.

In summary, the Netherlands is a naturist paradise, where the liberal and free-spirited atmosphere extends beyond mere acceptance of nudity. It's ingrained in the fabric of society. Naturism here isn't confined to hidden spots or exclusive clubs. Instead, it's a celebrated way of life that blends effortlessly with cultural, social, and recreational activities. Whether you're lounging on a tranquil beach, exploring vibrant cities, or joining a naturist community event, the Netherlands offers a welcoming embrace to all who seek the liberating experience of naturism.

Chapter 7:
Eastern Europe's Untamed Naturist Spots

Eastern Europe might not be the first place that comes to mind for naturist escapades, but it offers a rugged elegance that's hard to find elsewhere. Croatia's islands present secluded beaches, where the Adriatic Sea sparkles invitingly, making it an idyllic escape for naturists. Bulgaria's Black Sea coastlines offer a harmonious blend of wild beauty and rich history, perfect for those who enjoy a serene, undisturbed connection with nature. Venture into Hungary, where lakes and rivers stretch alongside sun-drenched glades, inviting you to immerse in a holistic naturist experience. In these corners of Europe, you'll discover inviting refuges that promise tranquility, natural freedom, and a captivating blend of cultures.

Croatia's Islands and Coastlines

Croatia, with its sprawling coastline and enchanting archipelagos, stands as a beacon for naturist enthusiasts. The Adriatic Sea laps gently against thousands of islands, each offering its own slice of untouched paradise. Few places rival Croatia for its seamless blend of natural beauty and liberated lifestyle. From the bustling island resorts to secluded coves, there's a naturist haven waiting for every type of traveler.

The island of Rab, often hailed as the birthplace of modern naturism in Croatia, is a must-visit. Its significance dates back to 1936 when King Edward VIII and Wallis Simpson first popularized nude bathing here. Rab's Kandalora Bay, affectionately known as the "English Beach," remains one of the most cherished naturist sites. Here, the azure waters meet pristine sands under the watchful eyes of ancient pine trees, offering both solace and a sense of history.

Heading further south, you'll discover the island of Hvar. Known for its sun-drenched days, the Pakleni Islands, just a short boat ride from Hvar, offer a series of pebbly beaches celebrated by naturists. Jerolim and Stipanska have distinct appeals—Jerolim for its tranquil, intimate settings, and Stipanska for its vibrant atmosphere and chic beach bars. Each makes it easy to transition from relaxation to socialization, all while basking in nature's glory.

In contrast, the island of Mljet remains a hidden treasure. Dominated by verdant forests and crystalline salt lakes, this island-laden national park is a sanctuary for naturist explorers. The Odysseus Cave offers a backdrop steeped in mythology, while the Soline Bay area allows for an undisturbed communion with nature. Mljet beckons the adventurous spirit, inviting you to uncover its mysteries.

A stone's throw away, the larger island of Cres exemplifies untouched beauty in the Adriatic. Its blend of rocky coastline and dense olive groves generates a sense of seclusion. The beaches of Sveti Ivan and Lubenice are pristine, with their turquoise bays offering naturists a perfect retreat. Diving into the clear waters or trekking through rugged terrains, Cres promises an immersive experience.

The mainland, too, hosts its own naturist gems. The Istrian Peninsula offers Valalta, one of Croatia's premier naturist resorts. Overlooking the Lim Channel, it's not just a beach but a sprawling property with all the amenities one might need—restaurants, pools, and sports facilities. Here, you can mingle with like-minded travelers or find your private nook to soak in the serene surroundings.

Dubrovnik, an iconic destination, has its fair share of naturist-friendly spots as well. Lokrum Island, a short ferry ride from the city's historic walls, becomes a naturist enclave during the summer months. Lokrum combines the allure of its botanical gardens and ancient ruins with crystal-clear bays perfect for a liberating dip.

Korčula, another jewel of the Dalmatian coast, holds the sandy beach of Lumbarda. This region, rich in vineyards and olive groves, provides naturists a unique blend of leisure and culinary delights. Wine tastings at local cellars followed by sunbathing on the golden shores make for an unforgettable experience.

As we venture into Southern Dalmatia, we arrive at the Elaphiti Islands, a relatively uncharted area for naturists. Beaches such as Sunj on Lopud Island offer gentle slopes into the sea, making it ideal for a relaxing day under the sun. The island's car-free environment enhances the tranquility, letting nature take center stage.

What sets Croatia apart is not just the sheer number of naturist locations, but the genuine acceptance and celebration of the lifestyle. Many of these destinations operate with official naturist designations, ensuring a respectful and welcoming environment. Local culture, entwined with a deep respect for nature and heritage, creates a unique backdrop for naturist travelers.

In Croatia, naturism isn't merely about sunbathing nude; it's about embracing a liberating ethos in one of Europe's most stunning settings. Whether you're exploring hidden coves by kayak, savoring local delicacies at beachfront taverns, or simply letting the day's end with a stunning Adriatic sunset, the islands and coastlines of Croatia provide the ideal canvas for a profound naturist experience.

Bulgaria's Black Sea Retreats

Nestled between the azure waves and lush green forests, Bulgaria's Black Sea coast is a hidden gem for naturists seeking a blend of relaxation and adventure. The coastline, spanning approximately 220 miles, offers a rich tapestry of landscapes—from golden sands and secluded coves to rugged cliffs and serene bays. As a naturist haven, Bulgaria provides an inviting environment where the harmony between nature and humanity can be truly celebrated.

Bulgaria's Black Sea retreats are an ideal destination for nature-lovers who appreciate the freedom to explore pristine environments without the constraints of clothing. The region boasts numerous naturist beaches, with Irakli, Vaya Beach, and Kamchia standing out among the best for their secluded beauty and tranquil settings. Each of these beaches offers a unique allure, inviting visitors to shed not only their clothes but also the stresses of daily life.

Irakli Beach, a long-time favorite among local and international naturists, is a perfect example of the idyllic beauty found along Bulgaria's coastline. Known for its soft sand and crystal-clear waters, the beach is part of a protected area that maintains its unspoiled nature. Here, the embrace of the sea and sun provides a liberating experience, as you find yourself surrounded by rolling dunes and wild flora. The remoteness of Irakli Beach makes it a sanctuary for those who seek peace and solace with nature.

Moving southwards, Vaya Beach offers a different yet equally enchanting naturist experience. Located near the ancient city of Sozopol, Vaya Beach combines historical charm with natural beauty. This beach is favored for its dramatic cliffs and expansive views of the Black Sea. The gentle waves lapping against the shore and the scent of the salty breeze create an atmosphere of serene detachment. The proximity to Sozopol adds an additional cultural layer to your stay, with its cobbled streets, wooden houses, and captivating history inviting further exploration.

Kamchia, another prominent naturist retreat, lies at the mouth of the Kamchia River, enveloped by thick forests and rich biodiversity. This area is a true haven for those who love both the sea and the forest, offering plentiful opportunities for hiking, bird-watching, and river excursions. The beach itself is less frequented, providing a more intimate setting for naturists to unwind in harmony with nature. The blend of freshwater and saltwater environments ensures a unique experience where the rhythmic sounds of the river and the sea create a soothing symphony.

Beyond these pristine beaches, Bulgaria's Black Sea coast is dotted with numerous smaller, lesser-known naturist spots, each with its own distinct character. Not far from the bustling city of Varna, you'll discover several secluded coves and bays that offer a quiet retreat from the more crowded beaches. The integration of modern amenities with natural beauty makes these spots ideal for day trips or weekend getaways, combining convenience with the desire to remain close to nature.

The local culture in Bulgaria is generally accepting and supportive of naturism, particularly in the designated areas. The openness of the community enhances the naturist experience, allowing visitors to integrate seamlessly with the local lifestyle. At the same time, it's essential to respect customs and be aware of the legal guidelines governing designated naturist zones. Familiarizing oneself with local etiquette ensures a pleasant and respectful experience for everyone involved.

One of the attractive aspects of Bulgaria's Black Sea retreats is the blend of natural beauty with local hospitality. Numerous family-run guesthouses and eco-lodges provide comfortable accommodations that cater specifically to naturist travelers. These establishments often offer amenities like private gardens, pools, and direct beach access, ensuring that the naturist philosophy extends beyond the beach and into your living space. The genuine warmth and friendliness of the Bulgarian hosts add a personal touch to your stay, making you feel welcome and at home.

The culinary scene in this region is another delightful aspect of the naturist experience. Coastal Bulgaria is known for its fresh seafood, seasonal vegetables, and rich wine heritage. Local markets and seaside taverns provide a taste of authentic Bulgarian cuisine, with dishes prepared using traditional recipes passed down through generations. Enjoying a meal under the open sky, with the sea breeze gently caressing your skin, creates an intimate connection with the local culture and the natural surroundings.

For adventurers, the Black Sea coast offers numerous activities that allow for an immersion in the rugged beauty of the region. From kayaking along the craggy shoreline to exploring the underwater world through snorkeling or diving, there's no shortage of ways to engage with nature actively. Those who prefer a more leisurely pace can partake in guided nature walks, photography tours, or simply bask in the sun, enveloped by the untouched beauty of the Bulgarian landscapes.

Nature conservation plays a pivotal role in maintaining the allure of Bulgaria's Black Sea retreats. Protected areas and efforts to preserve biodiversity ensure that these naturist havens remain pristine for future generations. Supporting local conservation initiatives is a meaningful way for visitors to contribute to the sustainability of these natural treasures. Engaging in eco-friendly practices, such as beach clean-ups or participating in wildlife monitoring programs, can enhance your connection to the environment and leave a positive impact.

Accessibility to Bulgaria's Black Sea retreats is relatively straightforward, with Varna and Burgas serving as key entry points.

Well-connected by flights and trains, these cities provide a gateway to the coastal naturist paradises. From there, car rentals or even local public transportation options can take you to your chosen retreat, allowing for a seamless transition from urban bustle to serene solitude.

Lastly, the vibrant seasons along the Black Sea coast offer different but equally captivating experiences throughout the year. The summers are warm and inviting, perfect for sunbathing and swimming, while the mild shoulder seasons—spring and autumn—bring a quieter, more reflective atmosphere. Even in winter, the stark beauty of the coastline can be enchanting, offering a peaceful escape for those who appreciate solitude and the raw elegance of nature.

In conclusion, Bulgaria's Black Sea retreats are a testament to the serenity and beauty that naturist destinations can offer. These spots provide an ideal blend of relaxation, adventure, culture, and nature, making them an essential experience for any naturist traveler. The allure of the Black Sea coast lies not only in its physical beauty but also in the emotional and spiritual freedom it provides. Whether you're a seasoned naturist or new to the lifestyle, exploring Bulgaria's Black Sea retreats promises an unforgettable journey of liberation and discovery.

Naturist Exploration in Hungary

Hungary, often overshadowed by its more famous European neighbors, holds its own with several naturist gems that captivate and invigorate the spirit. The country's landscape is as varied as its history, offering everything from forested mountains to vast plains, and, crucially, tranquil lakeside retreats that are perfect for naturists seeking a unique blend of relaxation and adventure. Hungary's rich cultural heritage subtly intertwines with the liberating ethos of naturism, creating a milieu where one can truly feel free and connected with nature.

One of Hungary's premier naturist sites is Lake Balaton, affectionately known as the "Hungarian Sea." As Central Europe's largest fresh-water lake, it boasts several officially sanctioned naturist beaches. The most well-known among them is the Balatonberény beach on the southwestern shore. This idyllic spot features golden sands, calm waters, and panoramic views of the surrounding hills. It's not just the physical beauty that makes Balatonberény special; there's an unspoken camaraderie amongst naturists here, a sense of communal freedom that stands at the core of the naturist experience.

A visit to Lake Balaton isn't complete without exploring the wellness aspect of naturism. Adjacent to many of these naturist spots, you'll find thermal baths—a staple of Hungarian culture. The Hévíz Thermal Lake, just a short drive from Balaton, is renowned worldwide. Imagine soaking in naturally warm, mineral-rich waters in the nude, surrounded by aquatic lilies and the gentle rustling of nearby trees. It's an experience that promises not just relaxation, but a deep sense of rejuvenation, making it a must for those who want to blend the joys of naturism with holistic wellness.

For those in search of a more secluded ambiance, the nearby village of Ábrahámhegy, located on the northern shore of Lake Balaton, offers a more intimate naturist beach. This smaller locale doesn't attract as many visitors, making it perfect for a peaceful retreat. Here, undisturbed stretches of pebbled shoreline meet the clear, inviting waters of Balaton. It's an excellent spot for both new and seasoned naturists looking to unwind and soak up some sun away from the more crowded areas.

Transport yourself away from the lake shores and into the heart of Hungary's countryside, and you'll find another haven: the Naturist Park in the Balaton Uplands National Park. This place is a naturist's dream, set amidst rolling hills, lush forests, and crystal-clear streams. It's not just a place for sunbathing; it's an exploration ground for hiking, bird-watching, and simply breathing in the fresh air of untouched nature. Activities like guided nature walks and forest baths are common, enhancing the holistic experience of connecting with the environment sans clothing.

Another remarkable site is the Naturista Oázis Kemping in Leányfalu, just north of Budapest along the Danube River. This naturist camping ground is well-known for its friendly atmosphere and pristine environment. Sheltered among trees, this campsite offers not only traditional camping spots but modern bungalows for those who prefer a bit more comfort. On-site amenities like swimming pools, saunas, and sports facilities ensure that visitors have plenty to do outside of traditional naturist pursuits. The proximity to the river also means opportunities for kayaking and paddleboarding—an exhilarating way to experience naturism in nature.

Don't overlook Budapest when considering naturist attractions. One might not immediately think of a bustling capital city as a naturist haven, but Budapest's thermal baths offer an urban twist on naturism. While not always strictly naturist, many of these historic baths have designated times or sections where clothing is optional. The Széchenyi Thermal Bath, the largest in Europe, is a notable example. Here, you can move from hot thermal pools to cool plunge pools and even enjoy outdoor lounging—all in the nude, if you visit during the right times. This juxtaposition of ancient architecture, bubbling thermal waters, and naturist freedom is an experience unlike any other.

Beyond these specific locales, it's essential to mention the broader naturist community in Hungary. This country boasts a warm and welcoming culture that could be surprising to those unfamiliar with Eastern Europe. Naturist clubs and organizations are active and engaging, frequently organizing events, excursions, and social gatherings that foster a sense of belonging. These groups are invaluable for new naturists who might want guidance and companionship as they explore this liberating lifestyle.

Hungary gleams as a naturist destination due to its picturesque settings and the harmonious blend of wellness, community, and nature. It invites one to shed the constraints of urban life—literally and figuratively—and immerse in a world where simplicity and freedom reign. Whether by the shores of Lake Balaton, in the serenity of forested national parks, or amidst the vibrant buzz of Budapest's historic baths, naturist exploration here promises an enriching and unforgettable journey. If you're looking to merge the beauty of Eastern Europe with the ethos of naturism, Hungary stands as an inviting, and somewhat hidden, treasure ready to be discovered.

Chapter 8:
Mediterranean Marvels for Naturists

Imagine the crystalline waters of the Mediterranean lapping against sun-kissed shores, where naturists can revel in the natural beauty and freedom of some of the world's most idyllic spots. Greece, with its serene isles like Crete and the enchanting Cyclades, offers perfect havens with secluded beaches and a welcoming ambience. Italy's enchanting shores, from the hidden spots in Sardinia to the lush retreats of Tuscany, present a romantic and liberating escape for naturists. Whether you're exploring ancient ruins or savoring delicious local cuisine, the Mediterranean's rich cultural tapestry and breathtaking landscapes create unforgettable experiences. Embrace the sun, sea, and sense of freedom that only these Mediterranean marvels can offer, making them a must-visit on your naturist travel itinerary.

Greece: Idyllic Isles

Imagine the pristine, sun-soaked shores of Greece, where ancient history meets modern naturist freedom on its idyllic isles. Each island offers unique experiences. The picturesque landscapes of Santorini, with their blue-domed churches, invite you to shed your inhibitions. Mykonos, known for its vibrant nightlife, provides a seamless blend of social nudity and festive spirit. In contrast, the tranquil beaches of Naxos cater to those seeking serene, uncluttered spaces for a more intimate connection with nature. These islands are not just destinations; they are sanctuaries for those who crave liberation, beauty, and historical richness in one breathtaking package.

Crete's Nude Coasts are a treasure trove of sun-soaked freedom, where the azure waters of the Mediterranean kiss the golden sands of this storied island. Nestled in the heart of the Mediterranean Sea, Crete offers naturist enthusiasts a sublime combination of rich history, vibrant culture, and, most importantly, a variety of breathtaking beaches where clothing is entirely optional.

First, let's journey to the western part of the island, where we find the world-famous *Red Beach*. Located near the vibrant town of Matala, Red Beach gets its name from the reddish hue of its sands, thanks to the unique volcanic rock formations that surround it. The hike to reach Red Beach is moderately challenging, adding a sense of anticipation for the stunning sight that awaits. As you step onto the beach, the sense of liberation is instantaneous, with sunbathers fully embracing the naturist lifestyle at this remote and scenic spot.

A few miles to the north, another fantastic destination is *Kommos Beach*. This expansive stretch of sand, once part of an ancient Minoan harbor, provides a more serene atmosphere compared to its neighboring beaches. Kommos is particularly popular among locals, and its secluded nature makes it a perfect spot for naturists seeking a peaceful escape. The nearby taverns offer a delightful mix of traditional Cretan cuisine and breathtaking views of the Libyan Sea. Kommos perfectly embodies the harmonious blend of culture and naturism that Crete offers.

Heading east, we find the lesser-known gem of *Filaki Beach*, situated on the south coast of Crete. This beach is nestled in a cove, surrounded by high cliffs that provide privacy and a shelter from the winds. The crystal-clear waters and the soft sand create an inviting haven for naturists. Filaki Beach is closely associated with the nearby Vritomartis Naturist Resort, one of the most esteemed naturist resorts in Greece. Staying at Vritomartis gives travelers the luxury of modern amenities while granting them easy access to this paradisiacal beach.

For those willing to venture even further, *Glyka Nera*, or Sweet Water Beach, is a hidden gem along the southern coast. Accessible mainly by boat or a rugged trail, the effort to reach Glyka Nera is well rewarded with pristine waters, partly shaded by tamarisk trees and freshwater springs. The water here is exceptionally clear, revealing a kaleidoscope of marine life below. It's a quiet retreat where sound carries no further than the whisper of the waves and the occasional chatter of contented naturists.

Exploring the northern coast, we encounter the beautiful and tranquil *Balos Lagoon*. Unlike the rugged seclusion of Glyka Nera, Balos offers striking contrasts of white sand and turquoise waters, framed by rocky cliffs. While Balos is not exclusively a naturist beach, its roomy expanse means you can find quieter spots where naturism is enjoyed. Don't miss the chance to hike to the viewpoint; the panoramic vista over the lagoon is nothing short of spectacular.

Moving to the northeast tip of Crete, *Vai Beach* combines pristine natural beauty with historical intrigue. Known primarily for its unique palm forest, Vai also provides secluded areas where naturists can bask in the sun. The palm forest, the largest of its kind in Europe, creates an exotic, almost surreal backdrop to your naturist experience. As you relax under the swaying palms, the boundary between Europe and a tropical paradise seems to blur magnificently.

One cannot discuss Crete's naturist scene without mentioning *Kedrodasos Beach*. Just a stone's throw away from the famous Elafonissi Beach, Kedrodasos is a hidden oasis that remains relatively untouched by the tourist masses. The beach is enveloped by a lush forest of cedar trees, offering both shade and a unique beauty. With its fine sands and crystal-clear waters, Kedrodasos is a naturist's sanctuary

— a place where you can truly connect with nature, both spiritually and physically.

Preveli Beach, located near the historic Preveli Monastery, is another location where naturism flourishes in a splendid natural setting. The beach is accompanied by a river that flows from the mountains into the sea, creating a natural lagoon ideal for a refreshing swim. The area is rich in both beauty and history; the palm forest, the river, and the sea all converge to create a captivating environment for your naturist adventures.

For a more communal experience, naturists can head to *Plakias Beach* on the southern coast. Plakias is one of the most naturist-friendly areas on Crete, with a significant portion of the beach dedicated to naturism. It's a place where you can easily meet like-minded travelers, exchange stories, and make lasting connections. The nearby village of Plakias offers accommodations, dining, and nightlife, making it an excellent base for those who seek a blend of relaxation and social activity.

Rounding off our tour, *Almyros Beach* near Agios Nikolaos offers both convenience and beauty for naturists. It's a spacious beach with fine sand and calm waters, making it ideal for families and solo travelers alike. The close proximity to Agios Nikolaos means you can seamlessly transition from the tranquility of the beach to the lively atmosphere of the town, enjoying the best of both worlds.

Crete's nude coasts offer a sensory feast and a gratifying sense of liberty for naturist travelers. Each beach, with its unique charm and characteristics, contributes to an unforgettable journey into the heart of naturist culture in the Mediterranean. The island's captivating landscapes, historical richness, and welcoming locals make Crete not just a destination, but an experience — a place where you can truly live and breathe in the essence of naturism.

Cyclades Cluster encompasses some of the most stunning and liberating naturist destinations in the Mediterranean. This Aegean Sea archipelago is more than a backdrop of tranquil beauty; it's a haven for those who seek the freedom of naturism. Each island offers its own unique charm, creating an unforgettable tapestry of experiences. From the white-washed buildings of Mykonos to the serene beaches of Paros, the Cyclades are a dream come true for naturists who wish to escape the conventional and embrace the extraordinary.

The magic of the Cyclades lies in their diversity. Let's start with Mykonos, often the first stop for many naturist travelers. Though renowned for its lively nightlife and cosmopolitan flair, Mykonos also boasts some hidden gems where nudism is embraced. Super Paradise Beach is a well-known spot where nudity is welcome, particularly at its eastern end. Here, you can let go of your inhibitions, bask in the warm Mediterranean sun, and swim in crystal-clear waters. While the beach can get crowded, it's a vivid reminder that naturism is as much about community as it is about solitude.

Just a short ferry ride away, you'll find the island of Paros. Paros offers a more relaxed vibe compared to Mykonos' fast-paced lifestyle. Paros beaches like Lageri and Monastiri are not officially designated for naturism, but they are widely accepted naturist spots. With their golden sands and translucent waters, these beaches allow you to lose yourself to the rhythmic sound of the waves and the whispering winds. It's a place where time seems to stand still, offering you the perfect opportunity to reconnect with nature and yourself.

And then there's beautiful Santorini. While Santorini's fame is largely attributed to its dramatic cliffs and iconic sunsets, it also offers secluded spots for naturism. Vlychada Beach, often referred to as "Moon Beach" due to its unique lunar-like landscape, is one such place where naturism is embraced. Wander along the black volcanic sands and bask in the natural wonders that surround you. The serenity of

Vlychada invites introspection and tranquility, allowing you to celebrate the art of naturism in an otherworldly setting.

Slightly off the beaten path, you'll discover Folegandros, an island that strikes a perfect balance between natural beauty and undisturbed solitude. Uncrowded beaches like Agali and Ambeli offer naturists an idyllic retreat where they can disrobe without worry. The rugged landscape is a stunning contrast to the smooth, inviting waters, and as the sun dips below the horizon, casting a golden hue over the land, you'll understand why Folegandros is a hidden gem in the Cyclades Cluster.

The more adventurous naturist will be drawn to the unspoiled island of Anafi. Anafi is a sanctuary for those who seek to be at one with the elements. Its beaches, such as Roukounas and Monastiri, are renowned for their natural, unmanicured beauty and their informal approach to naturism. This is a place where you can camp under the stars, wake up to the gentle sounds of the Aegean waves, and spend your days exploring both the rugged interior and the pristine coastline. Anafi invites a kind of raw, unplugged experience of naturism that can be both humbling and inspiring.

If you sail a bit further, you'll land on the shores of Naxos, the largest island in the Cyclades. Naxos merges history with pristine beaches, creating an enriching naturist experience. Plaka Beach, stretching for miles, is a favorite among naturists. Its powdery sand and clear, shallow waters make it perfect for long walks and peaceful swims. As you stroll along Plaka, you'll find that informal naturist sections blend seamlessly with areas where sunbathers are in traditional attire, embodying a spirit of coexistence and mutual respect.

The Cyclades Cluster also includes Syros, an island less frequented by tourists, making it an ideal spot for naturists seeking quieter locales. Armeos Beach in Galissas Bay is a hidden retreat where clothing is optional, and the atmosphere is relaxed. Surrounded by rocky outcrops and wild vegetation, the beach offers a private haven where you can truly unwind, far removed from the hustle and bustle of modern life.

Sifnos, famous for its culinary delights, also hosts a few naturist-friendly beaches that deserve a mention. One of the more well-known is the remote Fykiada Beach, situated in a beautiful bay that can be accessed via a scenic hiking trail or by boat. Fykiada's untouched natural beauty makes it a perfect naturist hideaway. The combination of serene waters and rugged terrain creates an enchanting backdrop for naturist activities, offering an escape that feeds both the body and the soul.

Serifos, with its rugged and untouched landscapes, boasts a more elusive and wild allure for naturists. Beaches like Agios Sostis and Vagia are less commercialized, presenting a raw and inviting spot for naturist travel. As you shed your clothes and step into the azure waters, you'll feel a profound connection to the ancient natural rhythms that have shaped the Cyclades for millennia. The simplicity and tranquility you find here can refresh your spirit, making it an unforgettable part of your naturist journey.

In the Cyclades, naturism is more than just a lifestyle choice; it's a way to experience the timeless beauty of these islands on a profoundly personal level. Each island in the cluster offers unique landscapes, rich histories, and the communal yet intimate experience that naturism provides. From the energetic Mykonos to the secluded Anafi, there's something for every type of naturist traveler in this Mediterranean paradise.

The broader understanding you gain on these islands transcends mere scenery; it's an education in freedom, beauty, and respect for nature and human diversity. These qualities make the Cyclades Cluster more than just a destination but a milestone in your naturist travel adventures. Embrace the journey, shed your reservations, and step into a world where the Aegean breeze whispers tales of ancient freedoms and modern-day wonders.

Italy: Enchanting Shores

Italy's enchanting shores beckon naturists with their blend of dramatic cliffs, serene beaches, and historical charm. Picture yourself exploring the pristine sands of Tuscany or uncovering the hidden gems along Sardinia's coastline, discovering secluded coves where the azure waters meet the untouched shoreline. Embrace the warm Mediterranean winds as you wander, the rich aroma of Italian cuisine lingering in the air. Whether you're an experienced naturist or a curious newcomer, Italy's landscape offers an idyllic escape that promises both relaxation and a deep connection to nature. It's here that you'll find a perfect harmony between the old-world romance and the liberating ethos of naturism.

Sardinia's Hidden Spots is where the sense of discovery mingles with the allure of undisturbed beauty. On this Mediterranean island, the landscape seamlessly oscillates between rugged mountains and serene beaches. Sardinia, with its turquoise waters and unspoiled terrain, offers naturists a canvas of tranquility and liberation. Some naturist spots here are well-known, yet many remain hidden treasures, waiting to be uncovered by adventurous travelers seeking solitude.

Perhaps the most enchanting quality of Sardinia is its ability to make you feel like an explorer in a forgotten paradise. Cale Genovese, tucked away on the northeastern coast, is a vibrant example of this. Hidden within a dramatic cliffside, the beach is accessed through narrow trails that weave through lush greenery. Only the intrepid manage to find their way here, rewarded with a stretch of sand where nature is the only bystander. It is a place where you can shed not only your clothes but also the stress that accumulates in the clothed world.

Travel further south, and you'd find Porto Ferro, a location embraced by ardent naturists for decades. Unlike Cale Genovese, Porto Ferro is relatively more accessible, yet its allure remains undiluted. The beach, with its deep golden sands and cerulean waves, is flanked by a fragrant pine forest. Exploring the trails around Porto Ferro can lead you to secluded nooks where you can bask in privacy. The sound of the sea, the scent of the forest, and the expansiveness of the horizon combine to create an immersive experience, allowing you to reconnect with nature and yourself.

While Porto Ferro and Cale Genovese are jewels in their own right, the ultimate naturist retreat in Sardinia might well be Cala Luna. Accessible primarily by boat or a challenging hike, Cala Luna boasts a dramatic landscape of limestone cliffs hugging a crescent-shaped bay. The beach serves as a natural amphitheater, echoing the whispers of the waves and the rustling of leaves. Here, the remoteness amplifies a sense of freedom. Stripped of societal expectations and enveloped by nature, one's connection to the earth feels profound and unfiltered.

To truly appreciate Sardinia's hidden naturist spots, it is essential to engage with local culture. The island's community prides itself on preserving their natural heritage and traditions. Small villages like Baunei and Dorgali near Cala Luna host local markets that provide a glimpse into the island's heart. Interacting with locals can enrich your experience, offering insights into the island's best-kept secrets and naturist-friendly locales not marked on tourist maps.

The western coast, albeit less frequented, equally deserves attention. Argentiera, once a thriving silver mining town, now embraces a quieter existence. The remnants of its industrial past juxtapose with the untouched beauty of its beaches. Naturism here feels like a reclamation of space, an act of transforming an old narrative into one of renewal and freedom. The seclusion of these beaches makes them ideal for naturists looking for a slice of history intertwined with raw nature.

For those who wish to blend naturist practices with outdoor adventures, the Gennargentu Mountains offer a perfect haven. These mountains, located in central Sardinia, cradle numerous hidden coves and valleys. Exploring the Gennargentu means miles of untouched wilderness where you can disrobe and immerse yourself in nature without encountering another soul. Hiking through these mountains will reveal hidden beaches and serene lakes, providing naturists with unparalleled seclusion and serenity.

The island's southern reaches showcase gems like Porto Sa Ruxi. Here, multiple small coves are separated by rocky outcrops, each a private sanctuary for sunbathing and swimming in the nude. The clear waters are ideal for snorkeling, revealing an underwater world as captivating as the landscape above. Stripping down here feels like peeling away layers of complexity, leaving only the primal joy of existing within nature.

Wherever you venture on Sardinia, the sensory experience is intoxicating. The feel of the warm sand underfoot, the caress of a Mediterranean breeze, and the sight of vivid sunsets paint a picture that lingers long after you leave. Sardinia's hidden naturist spots aren't just places; they are experiences that invite you to live more freely and deeply.

And if you want your naturist adventure to be even more enriching, integrate local gastronomy into your journey. Sardinia's cuisine is an enigma of flavors — from the salty pecorino cheeses to the sweet and saffron-infused seadas. Picnic under the expansive sky with these local delicacies, and your senses will be satiated in more ways than one.

Remember that the preservation of these hidden spots is paramount. Practicing sustainable naturism ensures that Sardinia's beauty remains unmarred for future visitors. Always carry out what you bring in, respect local customs, and tread lightly. This respect for nature fosters a symbiotic relationship — the land grants you freedom, and you, in turn, ensure its preservation.

Sardinia, with all its hidden spots, exemplifies the essence of naturism. It is a realm where you can exist in your most natural state, embraced by the landscape's raw beauty. Whether you find yourself on a secluded beach, a hidden cove, or a mountain trail, the island whispers a promise of liberation and connection. Discovering Sardinia's hidden spots isn't just about finding a place; it's about finding a piece of yourself, unconstrained and authentically free.

Tuscany Retreats evoke an image of rolling hills adorned with vineyards, olive groves, and medieval villages, all bathed in the warm glow of the Italian sun. But beyond its celebrated aesthetics, Tuscany has emerged as a haven for naturist travel enthusiasts in search of serene, liberating, and intimate vacation experiences. Imagine wandering through the countryside, liberated from the constraints of clothing, feeling the earth beneath your feet and the breeze against your skin. Tuscany beckons to the naturist traveler with its promise of connecting with nature in its purest form.

One of the most captivating aspects of a naturist retreat in Tuscany is the opportunity to immerse oneself in the region's rich cultural heritage. Picture yourself exploring an ancient Etruscan settlement or medieval castle, where history breathes through every stone. These explorations become uniquely personal when experienced in a state of undress, which many naturists find enhances their sense of freedom and connection to the past. Tuscany's naturist options often blend this historical allure with modern comfort, creating experiences that are both educational and rejuvenating.

An essential part of any naturist retreat in Tuscany is finding the perfect location. Fortunately, Tuscany offers an array of naturist-friendly accommodations and resorts. Properties like "Agriturismo Le Pianacce" provide a rustic yet luxurious escape, with private cottages surrounded by forests and hills. These venues often come equipped with wellness facilities like saunas and natural hot springs, where you can unwind and soak in the tranquil ambiance sans clothing.

While many visitors to Tuscany naturally gravitate towards famous cities like Florence and Pisa, naturist travelers might find more allure in the rural and coastal areas. Coastal retreats such as "Campo dei Fiori" offer breathtaking views of the Tyrrhenian Sea and secluded beaches perfect for nude sunbathing and swimming. Here, you can lose yourself in the rhythmic sounds of the waves, the vast horizon before you, and the feeling of being one with the elements.

The beautiful Tuscan landscapes are not just a feast for the eyes; they provide ideal settings for outdoor activities. Hiking through the Chianti region, cycling along the winding roads of the Val d'Orcia, or practicing yoga amidst fields of wildflowers are just some of the ways naturists can engage with Tuscany's natural beauty. These activities, performed without barriers, invite a deeper connection to the environment and an enhanced sense of physical and mental well-being.

In Tuscany, food and wine are as integral to the experience as the landscape itself. Naturist retreats often include farm-to-table dining experiences, allowing guests to enjoy the freshest local produce and artisanal products. Imagine participating in a communal meal in an open-air setting, savoring rich flavors while the warm Tuscan sun sets, casting golden hues over the vineyards. Pairing this gastronomic delight with local wines creates not just a meal, but a true celebration of the senses.

Community is another significant aspect of naturist retreats. Many venues host social events where travelers can meet like-minded individuals. Shared experiences, whether it's a guided tour of a nearby winery, a group hike, or a communal cooking class, foster connections that enhance the overall travel experience. In these inclusive environments, naturists can feel safe and supported, building friendships that often extend beyond the confines of the retreat.

For those seeking a more spiritual retreat, Tuscany offers several naturist-friendly wellness centers specializing in activities like meditation, art therapy, and even organic farming. The transformation that comes from participating in these activities while nude is profound. It strips away societal pressures and allows participants to focus purely on inner growth and connection to others. Tuscany's serene environment acts as a perfect backdrop for such spiritual journeys.

Interestingly, naturism in Tuscany is not a modern invention; it has historical roots. Ancient Romans and Etruscans, who once populated these lands, reputedly enjoyed communal bathing and nudity in certain contexts. Modern naturist sites in Tuscany often celebrate this aspect of history, offering visitors a sense of continuity and connection to the past. It's fascinating to think that the liberating experiences you enjoy today echo traditions thousands of years old.

Practical considerations are, of course, important as well. Tuscany's naturist resorts are well-equipped to cater to both rookie and seasoned naturists. They provide detailed guidelines and etiquettes to ensure everyone feels comfortable and respected. Moreover, accessibility is rarely an issue. Major naturist resorts are within easy reach of Tuscany's famous cities and landmarks, making it possible for travelers to enjoy both naturist and traditional tourist experiences during their stay.

Tuscany's climate is another advantage. The region enjoys a Mediterranean climate with hot summers and mild winters, making it an attractive destination for naturist travel year-round. The best time to visit for a naturist vacation is typically from late spring to early autumn when the weather is warm but not oppressively hot. Regardless of the season, the landscapes maintain their charm, acting as a constant invitation to commune with nature freely.

Ultimately, a naturist retreat in Tuscany offers more than just a vacation; it promises a rejuvenating journey of self-discovery and liberation. Whether you're unwinding in a luxurious, off-the-grid resort, exploring ancient ruins, or simply basking in the Tuscan sun, the freedom and joy of naturism elevates the entire experience. It's about finding a deeper appreciation of life, community, and the organic beauty that surrounds you. Tuscany stands as a testament to the endless possibilities for those daring enough to embrace naturism in one of the world's most enchanting settings.

Chapter 9:
Middle East Naturist Escapes

Stepping into the Middle East with expectations of naturist escapes may sound unconventional, but hidden gems such as Israel's secret beaches and the burgeoning naturism in Turkey invite the intrepid traveler to bask in a unique blend of ancient culture and liberating experiences. Imagine floating effortlessly in the Dead Sea, feeling the mineral-rich waters cradle your body in Israel, or discovering secluded coves along Turkey's stunning coastline, where history whispers through ancient ruins and pristine sands invite you to shed the last vestige of restraint. These destinations offer a compelling mix of raw, natural beauty and a burgeoning naturist scene that embraces freedom and personal liberation. Every moment spent here becomes an intimate dance between you and the timeless landscapes, promising memories that linger long after the journey ends.

Israel's Secret Beaches

The Middle East, with its vibrant history and rich tapestry of cultures, is often overlooked by those seeking naturist experiences. Yet, hidden within Israel's sun-drenched coastline lie some of the most pristine and secluded beaches, perfect for those seeking a liberating escape. These secret beaches offer a blend of unspoiled nature and discreet privacy, making them ideal for naturists.

Israel's coastline stretches over 170 miles along the Mediterranean Sea, providing ample opportunities for secluded beachfronts. While not all of these locales are officially recognized as naturist beaches, there are several lesser-known spots where discretion meets natural beauty, creating the perfect haven for a naturist.

One such hidden gem is Ga'ash Beach, located just south of Natanya. Nestled beneath the rugged cliffs, this beach provides a natural barrier against the outside world. The untouched sand and crystal-clear waters invite visitors to shed their clothes and bask in the sun's warmth, feeling utterly free. The relatively remote location ensures a peaceful environment, free from prying eyes, where one can connect with nature in its purest form.

Further south, you'll find the tranquil Shavit Beach near Ashdod. This spot, which is often frequented by local naturists, maintains a serene and friendly atmosphere. The gentle waves lapping against the shore harmonize with the soft whispers of the wind, creating a soundtrack of pure relaxation. Visitors can enjoy long walks along the coastline, feeling the smooth sand beneath their feet, and watching the sun set in a blaze of colors as it dips below the horizon.

The beauty of Israel's secret beaches also lies in their natural surroundings. Ein Bokek Beach, near the Dead Sea, is a short drive from the more famous tourist sites. Here, the stark contrast between the mineral-rich waters and the desert background creates a striking and almost surreal setting. The therapeutic properties of the Dead Sea are renowned, and soaking in its waters, unfettered by swimsuits, can be both healing and profoundly peaceful.

And then there's Apollonia Beach, bordered by the remnants of an ancient fortress. The combination of historical intrigue and sun-warmed sand creates a unique setting. This shoreline whispers secrets of the past, which mingle with the present-day liberating experience of naturism. Wandering among the ancient ruins, you can almost feel a connection with the generations past who may have also sought solace and freedom here.

These hidden treasures of Israel are often discovered through local knowledge and word-of-mouth, adding an element of adventure to the naturist experience. The trail to these beaches is an exploration in itself—winding paths, hidden routes, and the thrill of finding a perfect, untouched strand of sand where you can simply be.

Accessibility varies, and it's sometimes necessary to trek a bit off the beaten path. However, the reward is immense for those willing to venture beyond the conventional tourist spots. Exploring these beaches with respect for their natural state ensures they remain pristine for future visitors.

Practical advice for naturist travelers in Israel includes bringing sufficient supplies for your visit, as these beaches usually lack commercial facilities. Packing essentials such as water, snacks, and sun protection is crucial. Additionally, understanding that naturism is not widespread in Israel can help in managing expectations and ensuring respectful and discreet behavior to avoid conflicts.

For the seasoned naturist, Israeli culture offers a fascinating melting pot of traditions and modernity. Engaging with this blend through the lens of naturism can provide a multi-faceted travel experience. Conversations with locals may reveal more hidden spots or cultural insights; the warmth and hospitality often come with an open-minded curiosity about lifestyles different from their own.

Visiting Israel's secret beaches isn't just about soaking up the sun in the nude; it's about immersing oneself in an experience where history, nature, and the sense of freedom intertwine. These secluded spots offer a haven for self-discovery and relaxation, removing the barriers between oneself and the world. Naturists here can feel a part of something larger—the ebb and flow of tides, the timelessness of nature, and the ancient stories upon the winds.

If you're planning a naturist journey to the Middle East, Israel's secret beaches beckon with the promise of untouched beauty and tranquil solitude. Whether you're a seasoned naturist or new to the experience, these hidden gems provide the perfect backdrop for a liberating and rejuvenating adventure unlike any other. As you leave these shores, the memories of the soft sands, gentle waves, and boundless freedom will invite you to return time and again.

naturism in turkey

Turkey, situated where East meets West, offers a unique experience for naturist travelers. The country's rich cultural heritage, diverse landscapes, and intriguing history provide a setting that is both liberating and inspiring for those eager to explore naturism in a new and different context.

In Turkey, naturism isn't mainstream or widely advertised, though pockets of serene nudist havens do exist. Several culturally sensitive factors come into play given Turkey's predominantly Muslim population and conservative leanings. However, with a bit of research and respect for local customs, it's possible to find secluded spots that provide a naturist experience surrounded by breathtaking beauty.

A significant example is Patara Beach, located along Turkey's southwestern coast on the Mediterranean. Known for its expansive sand dunes, ancient ruins, and crystalline waters, Patara Beach holds a magical allure for naturists. While nudity isn't officially sanctioned, the vastness of the beach allows you to find quieter spots where you can discreetly enjoy the naturist lifestyle. The breathtaking scenery makes it a perfect escape for those seeking solitude and connection with nature.

Kabak Bay, another hidden gem, offers a more intimate experience with nature. Nestled among pine forests and mountains, this secluded bay remains a sanctuary for those searching for peace and tranquility. Accessible via a scenic hike, it's rewarded with pristine beaches and clear waters. While not exclusively naturist, the remoteness of Kabak allows for a sense of freedom and privacy that can be harnessed for a naturist experience.

On the Aegean shores, visit the Dikili region, specifically Bademli and Kalem Island. Bademli, a small village, and Kalem Island are ideal locations for those seeking an undisturbed naturist experience. They offer secluded coves and a dreamy atmosphere infused with the aromatic scents of olive groves and pine trees. The area's low tourist traffic means naturists can find calm sanctuary here, far from the rush of conventional beach destinations.

The allure of Turkey doesn't entirely rest on its natural beaches alone. Historical wonders and cultural sites impart a romantic essence for any traveler. Walking among the ruins of Ephesus or gazing over the mystical landscapes of Cappadocia enriches the journey and adds depth to your naturist escape. These storied landscapes enhance the overall feelings of liberation and wonder uniquely tied to naturism.

For those who prefer a more structured experience, there's the possibility of renting private villas or secluded guest houses in regions renowned for their natural beauty such as the Lycian Way or Turquoise Coast. Many such accommodations offer private pools and gardens where naturism can be joyfully practiced in complete seclusion. Always communicate openly with property owners to confirm their comfort with naturist practices, ensuring mutual respect and understanding.

Cultural sensitivity remains paramount in Turkey. It's essential to be aware that public nudity can be met with disapproval, and therefore, discretion is key. Opting for secluded spots and acting respectfully toward local communities and customs not only ensures a pleasant experience but also fosters goodwill. Nude swimming or sunbathing should be reserved for out-of-the-way beaches where privacy can be maintained, avoiding densely populated areas.

Cappadocia, while not typically associated with naturism, offers a different kind of personal escape. The ethereal landscape, with its hot air balloon rides and majestic valleys, may not offer explicit naturist opportunities, but the sheer sense of freedom it inspires can be just as liberating. This region's vastness and natural architecture provide solitude, making it possible to find private corners for meditation or naturist experiences under the open sky.

Indeed, Turkey's blend of natural beauty, cultural richness, and historical significance create a unique backdrop for those yearning for a naturist escape that goes beyond the conventional beach experience. The harmony between the world's oldest civilizations and stunning landscapes encourages an exploration that is both inward and outward, making your naturist journey in Turkey unforgettable and sublimely enriching.

In conclusion, while Turkey may not boast a broad spectrum of established naturist venues, the opportunities to embrace naturism discreetly and respectfully are plentiful for the discerning traveler. By exploring lesser-known spots and understanding the cultural sensitivities, you can experience the freedom of naturism amidst some of the world's most captivating settings. The journey through Turkey will undoubtedly leave an indelible mark on your spirit, blending naturism with an appreciation for the diverse wonders this ancient land has to offer.

Chapter 10:
Africa's Untapped Naturist Treasures

Africa is a continent rich in diversity and teeming with hidden gems for the adventurous naturist. From the breathtaking landscapes of South Africa, where the untouched wilderness meets the expansive ocean, to the emerging naturist scene in Morocco, characterized by its vibrant culture and welcoming communities, Africa offers an array of liberating experiences. Imagine shedding your clothes under the African sun, surrounded by the majestic beauty of nature, feeling a profound connection to the land and its people. This chapter will guide you through untouched beaches, secluded retreats, and the unique cultural encounters awaiting those willing to explore Africa's naturist frontiers, promising not just a vacation, but a soulful journey into the heart of a magical and uncharted territory.

South Africa: Wild and Free

In the heart of Africa's treasures lies a land as diverse as it is enchanting: South Africa. Often synonymous with spectacular landscapes and vibrant cultures, it also boasts a remarkable range of naturist options that seamlessly blend freedom and natural beauty. South Africa is not just a destination; it's an experience that connects you to nature in the most liberating way.

South Africa's naturist offerings are as varied as its topography, from pristine beaches along the coastline to secluded spots in the wild. The country's naturally open spirit extends to its naturist culture, where visitors can find spaces that promote both relaxation and adventure. One of the well-loved naturist beaches is Sandy Bay, located near Cape Town. Here, the scenic beauty of rugged cliffs meets the expansive blue of the ocean, creating a perfect backdrop for a naturist visit. It's a place where you can let go of all constraints and immerse yourself fully in the spectacular surroundings.

Another gem in South Africa's naturist crown is the Harmony Nature Farm, situated in Gauteng. This tranquil retreat offers a unique combination of naturist freedom and the rustic charm of the African bush. Walking through its serene paths, you might encounter an array of local wildlife, making it one of the most unique naturist experiences you can imagine. The experience at Harmony Nature Farm is designed to be interactive, letting visitors join group walks, game drives, or simply unwind by the pool in a rustic but comfortable environment.

For those inclined towards more luxurious settings, the SunEden Naturist Resort provides both comfort and a close-knit community feel. Located near Pretoria, SunEden is an oasis of relaxation, featuring various amenities such as swimming pools, spas, and even hiking trails where one can enjoy the natural surroundings. The resort promotes a laid-back atmosphere where friendships blossom, and life seems to slow down, allowing guests to appreciate every moment without the constraints of clothing.

The spirit of South Africa is not just about individual freedom but also about communal experiences. Events like the annual South African Naturist Federation (SANFED) gatherings exemplify this. These events bring together naturists from all walks of life, promoting a sense of community and shared experiences that further enrich your visit. From group hikes to communal meals, these gatherings make naturism more than just a personal liberation—it becomes a collective celebration.

South Africa's naturist spots also offer a chance to engage with the local culture, as many of these places are close to cultural and historical sites. For example, spending time at a naturist retreat near Johannesburg allows you the freedom to explore the city's rich history and vibrant arts scene. Combining naturism with cultural tourism offers a dual experience of introspection and external discovery, making your journey even more enriching.

The Eastern Cape's Wild Coast is another fantastic destination for naturists. Known for its untamed beauty, this region provides an almost poetic sense of freedom. Here, nature is untouched, and the sparsely populated beaches become your own private paradise. The Wild Coast's remoteness makes it ideal for those seeking to disconnect from the bustling life and reconnect with nature on an intimate level. The sense of solitude here amplifies the naturist experience, making every moment feel like a profound communion with the Earth.

For naturist travelers who enjoy a bit of adventure, South Africa's landscapes offer endless possibilities. Imagine hiking through the Drakensberg Mountains, marveling at the dramatic cliffs and lush valleys. These hikes can be even more rewarding when enjoyed in the nude, as the freedom of naturism allows for a more immersive experience in nature. The feeling of trekking through diverse terrains while entirely unencumbered is both exhilarating and grounding, fostering a deeper connection to the natural world.

Health and wellness enthusiasts will find South Africa's naturist destinations perfect for activities such as yoga and meditation. Many resorts and retreats offer yoga sessions in serene natural settings, where the absence of clothing helps to deepen the practice. Imagine a sunrise yoga session with the sound of waves crashing in the background or meditating in the middle of the bush, surrounded by the whispering sounds of wildlife. These experiences can be profoundly transformative, offering not just relaxation but a deep sense of spiritual renewal.

Besides personal enjoyment, visiting South Africa's naturist locales also plays a role in supporting local communities. Many naturist resorts and retreats employ local staff and source their supplies from nearby farms, promoting sustainability and aiding the local economy. By choosing these destinations, you not only enrich your own experience but also contribute positively to the places you visit, ensuring that these natural havens continue to flourish.

It's important to note that understanding local customs and legalities related to naturism is crucial when planning your trip. South Africa has specific regions where naturism is more accepted and institutions like SANFED work to guide and inform visitors about the best practices to ensure a respectful and enjoyable experience. Being mindful of these guidelines helps in preserving the integrity of naturist spots and promotes a positive relationship between naturists and local communities.

The best time to visit South Africa for a naturist adventure is during the summer months from November to March. The weather is warm and ideal for outdoor activities, although certain areas along the coast can be enjoyed year-round due to their moderate climates. Planning your visit around these months not only ensures the best weather but also aligns with various naturist events and gatherings, enhancing your overall experience.

A naturist journey to South Africa is unlike any other; it's a dance of freedom and nature, a blend of relaxation and adventure. Whether you're lounging on the sandy shores of Cape Town, hiking the rugged trails of the Drakensberg, or immersing yourself in the warm community at a resort, South Africa offers a myriad of naturist experiences that are bound to leave an indelible mark on your soul. Here, in the heart of Africa's untapped naturist treasures, you'll find not just a destination but a sense of liberation as wild and free as the land itself.

Morocco's Emerging Scene

As we turn our sights to Morocco, envision rolling sand dunes, bustling souks, and enchanting Berber villages. But there's a side to Morocco that's slowly capturing the attention of the naturist community. Known for its majestic landscapes and rich cultural tapestry, Morocco offers more than just a traditional tourist experience. Here, naturism is beginning to find its place, quietly and respectfully weaving itself into the fabric of Moroccan hospitality.

Morocco's cultural conservatism might come to mind, making it a surprising entry on an exploration of naturist destinations. However, the emerging scene is discreet and respects local customs, allowing for a unique blend of freedom and tradition. Naturism in Morocco isn't about brash exhibitions, but rather about connecting intimately with nature in places where it's welcomed.

One must tread cautiously, yet with an open heart, to partake in Morocco's blossoming naturist offerings. The first glimmers of naturism can be found in niche resorts and secluded beach hideaways, where the emphasis is on privacy and intimacy with the natural world. These spaces are not widely advertised; they are shared among the community, discovered through word-of-mouth and trusted naturist networks.

The southern coast of Morocco, particularly around the city of Agadir, offers some of the most promising opportunities. With its expansive beaches and inviting Atlantic waters, the environment naturally lends itself to naturist relaxation. There are pockets along this coast where naturist practices are accepted, often within the confines of private resorts designed specifically with naturist guests in mind.

In these settings, naturists can sunbathe, swim, and engage in beach sports without the confines of clothing, all while enjoying the awe-inspiring Moroccan landscapes. The presence of these resorts points to a growing acceptance and interest in naturism among tourists and locals, showcasing how cultural boundaries can be navigated and respected.

For those more adventurous, the desert offers a different kind of naturist retreat. Imagine stripping away not just your clothes, but the hustle and bustle of daily life, under the vast, star-studded Saharan sky. Some eco-lodges and desert camps, operating on principles of minimal environmental impact and profound natural connection, welcome naturist practices. These experiences are often combined with camel treks, sandboarding, and oasis picnics, creating a holistic and serene naturist experience.

Of course, this doesn't mean naturism is broadly accepted across the country. Morocco's legal framework and societal norms still align closely with traditional modesty standards. Naturist travelers must exercise discernment and respect, ensuring their practices do not offend or infringe upon local sensibilities. This balance of respect and liberation is what makes Morocco's naturist scene both challenging and rewarding to explore.

A further extension of this emerging scene can be found in Morocco's emphasis on wellness and holistic retreats. The natural beauty of Morocco, from the Atlas Mountains to its serene coastal towns, offers the perfect backdrop for a range of wellness activities – yoga, meditation, and more. Some progressive wellness retreats are beginning to incorporate clothing-optional policies in specified areas, catering to those who find attunement with their inner selves and surroundings in the absence of clothing.

For naturist tourists in Morocco, preparation is key. Research and connecting with local naturist societies or international naturist communities can provide valuable insights and recommendations. Often, the best naturist spots in Morocco are not the ones splashed across glossy travel brochures but those whispered about in naturist forums or shared through trusted networks.

In conclusion, Morocco's emergence as a naturist destination is a testament to the evolving nature of global travel. It's about finding common ground, appreciating the stunning backdrop Morocco provides, and engaging in naturism in a way that is sensitive to and respectful of local traditions. With careful planning and an open heart, Morocco can be a place where naturists find both adventure and tranquility, all while contributing to a burgeoning community that values nature, freedom, and respect.

Chapter 11: Asia's Hidden Naturist Paradises

Venturing into Asia reveals a treasure trove of hidden naturist paradises, where the lush landscapes and serene beaches offer a perfect backdrop for the naturist lifestyle. Thailand, with its exotic charm, beckons with spots like Phuket's nude getaways and the secluded sanctuaries of Koh Samui. Meanwhile, India is emerging as a haven for naturists, with Goa's open beaches and the picturesque Kerala backwaters offering idyllic escapes. These destinations, steeped in rich culture and natural beauty, provide a unique blend of liberation and tranquility. Whether you seek the thrill of new frontiers or the peace of untouched nature, Asia's naturist paradises promise an unforgettable journey.

Thailand: Exotic Freedom

Thailand, the Land of Smiles, offers a unique blend of cultural richness and naturist freedom, making it an unparalleled destination for naturist travelers. Nestled in the heart of Southeast Asia, this exotic paradise harmoniously melds the freedom to be oneself with the allure of pristine beaches and lush tropical landscapes. Imagine walking along secluded stretches of white sand, the warm ocean breeze caressing your skin as you enjoy the mesmerizing views of turquoise waters. Thailand's naturist destinations, such as the tranquil spots in Phuket and the serene corners of Koh Samui, are as welcoming as they are breathtaking, offering a liberating escape from the everyday. Whether you're exploring hidden coves or experiencing the vibrant local culture, Thailand promises an unforgettable naturist adventure where your sense of freedom and connection to nature can truly flourish.

Phuket's Nude Getaways is an absolute paradise for those who seek the freedom of naturist travel in a setting of sheer beauty and tropical charm. Phuket, Thailand's largest island, is not only known for its bustling nightlife and splendid beaches but also for its lesser-known naturist-friendly spots that offer an escape from the ordinary. Whether you're a seasoned naturist or new to the lifestyle, Phuket's nude getaways promise a liberating experience that's hard to match.

Imagine waking up to the sound of waves gently lapping the shore, the sun casting golden hues across the crystal-clear waters. At some of Phuket's hidden naturist resorts, this isn't a dream—it's a daily reality. One such gem is the *Barefoot Resort*, nestled in a secluded part of the island where privacy is paramount. Here, you can shed your clothes and inhibitions alike, basking in the sun by the infinity pool or taking leisurely walks on the private stretch of beach. The resort's eco-friendly philosophy ensures that your stay is not only freeing but also in harmony with nature.

For those who love a bit of adventure, Phuket offers more than just tranquil resorts. *Banana Beach* is a must-visit for the adventurous naturist. Reached by boat or a challenging hike through lush greenery, this beach remains largely untouched by mass tourism. The azure waters and soft, white sands make it perfect for snorkeling, sunbathing, or simply enjoying the natural beauty sans clothing. While Banana Beach isn't officially naturist, its isolation makes it a haven for those who prefer to swim and sunbathe in the nude.

Another spot worth mentioning is the naturist community at *Hidden Beach Resort*, found near the southern tip of Phuket. This resort caters specifically to naturists and offers a range of accommodations, from quaint bungalows to luxurious villas. Besides the breathtaking beach, the resort provides yoga sessions, meditation classes, and even naturist massages—all designed to enhance your sense of peace and well-being. The communal dining experience here is an excellent opportunity to connect with fellow naturists from around the world, sharing stories and experiences under the open sky.

The beauty of Phuket doesn't end at its beaches. The island is surrounded by smaller islets, many of which are perfect naturist escape points. A short boat ride can take you to the *Coral Island*, known locally as Koh Hae. Though popular with day-trippers, the far end of the island often remains quiet and offers an unspoiled spot for naturist adventures. Pristine coral reefs make it a remarkable place for snorkeling, where you can float freely among the vibrant marine life.

For naturists who appreciate a sense of culture alongside their beach escapes, the *Phuket Old Town* offers a fascinating contrast. Stroll through the historic streets, adorned with Sino-Portuguese architecture, and indulge in the local cuisine at its many open-air markets and street stalls. While it's essential to dress appropriately in town out of respect for local customs, the transition back to naturist enclaves is quick, allowing you to enjoy the best of both worlds.

Phuket's warm and welcoming naturist scene isn't limited to specific resorts and beaches. The island's relaxed atmosphere extends to its numerous wellness retreats, where yoga and meditation sessions encourage a harmonious connection with the natural world. These retreats often host naturist-friendly events and workshops, allowing you to deepen your practice without the constraints of clothing, thus enhancing the overall experience. Engaging in mindful activities not only rejuvenates the body but also nurtures the spirit, making your naturist vacation truly transformative.

However, while Phuket may seem like a naturist's dream, it's crucial to navigate the local legalities and customs with care. Thailand is a conservative country, and understanding the nuances of naturist-friendly areas versus public spaces is essential. Always seek out designated naturist resorts and secluded beaches, and avoid public nudity outside these areas to respect local traditions and maintain a positive image of the naturist community.

In conclusion, Phuket offers a diverse range of experiences for the naturist traveler. From serene, hidden beaches and exclusive resorts to vibrant cultural explorations, the island promises a blend of relaxation, adventure, and connection with nature. Whether you're soaking in the sun on a secluded beach, engaging in wellness practices at a naturist retreat, or exploring the rich cultural tapestry of Phuket Old Town, each moment is an invitation to rediscover the joy of being unabashedly yourself. So pack light, leave your worries behind, and let Phuket's nude getaways be the next stop on your naturist journey.

Koh Samui Seclusions offers an unrivaled escape into a world of serene beauty and untouched nature. Situated in the Gulf of Thailand, Koh Samui stands as a beacon for those who seek solace and a liberating experience away from the hustle and bustle of city life. Nudists will find a sanctuary here, where the relaxed atmosphere perfectly complements the naturist ethos of freedom and authenticity. Imagine waking up to the gentle sound of waves, with nothing but the pristine sands and turquoise waters stretching before you. This is a place where you can truly breathe and reconnect with both nature and yourself.

The island's diverse landscape presents a myriad of opportunities for naturist activities. Secluded beaches, hidden by lush greenery and towering palms, offer a private paradise where you can fully immerse yourself in the naturist lifestyle. Whether you're a seasoned naturist or a curious newcomer, Koh Samui's inviting environment makes it easy to shed your clothes and any inhibitions. For those who cherish the feeling of the sun kissing their skin and the breeze tousling their hair, the island's uncrowded shores deliver an experience that's both intimate and liberating.

Take the time to explore the numerous bays and coves that dot the coastline. Among the most recommended for naturists is Silver Beach, known locally as Haad Thong Ta-khian. Tucked away between Lamai and Chaweng, this beach is less trafficked and provides a spectacularly scenic backdrop for a day of sunbathing in the nude. The soft, powdery sands and calm, clear waters make it an ideal spot to unwind and forget the stresses of the outside world. Here, you can luxuriate in the simplicity of life, with a good book or a gentle swim in the warm sea.

While Silver Beach is a standout, you'll also find other secluded spots where you can practice naturism freely. Coral Cove Beach, another lesser-known gem, is perfect for those looking to escape the more populous areas. It offers a quiet haven where you can enjoy snorkeling, revealing a vibrant underwater world that's as captivating as the views above the surface. Walking along the untouched shores, you'll find that the sense of isolation and peace enhances the naturist experience, echoing the primal connection between human and nature.

The allure of Koh Samui isn't limited to its beaches; the island's lush interior is teeming with natural wonders waiting to be explored. Embark on a hike through the jungle-clad hills or visit one of the many waterfalls, such as the famous Na Muang Waterfalls. Here, the landscape transforms from sun-soaked sand to verdant greenery, offering a different kind of retreat. The experience of stripping down and feeling the rush of cool, fresh water from the falls on your skin is invigorating and memorable.

For those who enjoy a blend of socializing and solitude, there are naturist resorts on Koh Samui that cater specifically to a naturist clientele. These resorts often provide a range of amenities designed to enhance your stay, from lush garden settings, private pools, and communal dining areas where you can enjoy meals in a naturist-friendly environment. Such settings foster a sense of community while respecting personal space and privacy, allowing you to engage with like-minded individuals or retreat into peaceful seclusion as you desire.

One of the most well-regarded resorts is Orient Resort and Spa, located near the more tranquil parts of the island. This naturist haven offers beautifully appointed bungalows, a friendly atmosphere, and a range of activities to keep you engaged. Whether you choose to indulge in a traditional Thai massage, partake in a yoga class, or simply lounge by the pool, the resort is designed to provide a holistic and unencumbered experience.

Adventurous souls may wish to take to the waters around Koh Samui. Kayaking through the crystal-clear seas or embarking on a boat trip to nearby islands like Koh Phangan and Ang Thong Marine Park presents more secluded spots for naturist exploration, with breathtaking scenery and abundant marine life. Imagine setting sail in the early morning, the sun gradually warming the day, and finding a deserted beach where you can enjoy the freedom of naturism in complete solitude.

Cultural experiences also abound on Koh Samui. While naturism and local customs need to be balanced respectfully, there are numerous temples and markets worth visiting. When exploring non-naturist areas, it's essential to adhere to appropriate dress codes and be mindful of cultural sensitivities. The famous Big Buddha Temple, Wat Phra Yai, is a must-see, not only for its impressive 12-meter statue but for the panoramic views it offers of the island and sea.

Food is an integral part of the Koh Samui experience. Savor the fresh flavors of Thai cuisine at local eateries, indulge in sumptuous seafood straight from the ocean, or perhaps take a cooking class to learn the secrets of Thai cooking. Many naturist-friendly resorts offer classes where clothing is optional, making the culinary journey both educational and liberating.

As day turns to evening, the island's laid-back vibe makes for enchanting nights. Picture yourself dining al fresco under a canopy of stars, the gentle lapping of waves providing the perfect soundtrack. Beachside bars and restaurants often have live music, creating an ideal atmosphere for relaxation and reflection on the day's adventures.

Koh Samui Seclusions presents an idyll for the naturist traveler—an island that harmonizes natural beauty and a liberating spirit. Here, you can immerse yourself in the untouched landscapes, engage with both the environment and the culture, and create memories that will last a lifetime. It's a destination that invites you to shed the layers of modern life and return to a state of pure, unadulterated freedom. Embrace the seclusion, the beauty, and the boundless possibilities of Koh Samui.

India: Emerging Spots

India, with its diverse landscape and rich cultural heritage, is gradually unveiling itself as a promising haven for naturists seeking new adventures. While the concept of naturism is still gaining traction here, places like Goa and Kerala are at the forefront of this emerging trend. Goa's sun-kissed beaches offer a relaxed atmosphere where free-spirited travelers can embrace the freedom of being one with nature. The serene backwaters of Kerala, on the other hand, provide a tranquil escape, perfect for those looking to rejuvenate in a natural setting. As the country's naturist spots continue to gain popularity, India promises not only breathtaking locales but also a unique cultural experience, making it an enticing addition to any naturist's travel itinerary.

Goa's Open Beaches Goa's open beaches are a beacon for naturists seeking freedom and connection with nature in India. With its golden sands, translucent waters, and verdant backdrops, Goa's beaches offer an ideal haven for those embracing naturism. One of the most compelling features of these beaches is their openness. The inviting stretches of coastline are perfect for those who wish to soak up the sun without the constraints of swimwear.

Exploring Goa's beaches, you encounter a unique blend of tranquility and excitement. Some of the more popular spots, like Arambol and Anjuna, have sections where naturists can feel at ease. The relaxed, bohemian vibe that permeates the air is palpable, attracting a diverse crowd of free-spirited individuals. Here, you can engage in enriching conversations with fellow travelers or simply bask in the calming presence of the ocean.

Taking a stroll along these open beaches in the early morning or late afternoon reveals their true magic. Soft light filters through the coconut palms, casting a serene glow on the sand. The gentle lapping of the waves creates a symphony of natural sounds that soothe the soul. It's not uncommon to spot others practicing yoga, meditating, or engaging in other mindful activities, creating a sense of communal serenity.

One of the profound pleasures of naturism in Goa is the opportunity to connect with nature on an intimate level. The feeling of the warm sun on your skin, the breeze as it dances across the water, and the textures of the sand beneath your feet—all contribute to a sensory experience that celebrates simplicity and freedom. This immersion in the natural world fosters a deep sense of well-being and rejuvenation.

Beyond the physical pleasures, naturism on Goa's open beaches also allows for cultural exploration. Goa's rich history as a Portuguese colony has left an indelible mark on its culture, visible in the architecture, cuisine, and lifestyle of its inhabitants. As you wander the beaches and nearby towns, you're likely to encounter charming churches, colorful markets, and tantalizing street food. These encounters offer a delightful contrast to the natural splendor of the beaches, enriching your travel experience.

While Goa's open beaches offer a relaxed environment, it's important to be mindful of local customs and regulations. In certain areas, naturism is more accepted and practiced openly, while in others, it might be met with less enthusiasm. Respect for local culture and sensitivity to the environment is key to ensuring a positive experience. Always follow posted guidelines and seek out areas known for their naturist-friendly policies.

Arambol Beach stands out as a favored spot among naturists. Known for its eclectic mix of visitors, vibrant art scene, and wellness activities, Arambol creates an inviting atmosphere for naturist enthusiasts. The beach stretches for miles, offering ample space to find a secluded spot where you can relax and unwind. The nearby Sweet Water Lake, with its lush greenery and serene waters, provides a perfect spot for a refreshing dip.

Anjuna Beach, another gem, is renowned for its lively flea market and legendary full-moon parties. During the day, naturists can find secluded sections of the beach to enjoy the sun and sea. As the sun sets, the beach transforms into a hub of music and dance, creating a vibrant blend of relaxation and excitement. This dynamic environment allows you to enjoy the best of both worlds—serenity by day and celebration by night.

For those seeking a more tranquil experience, Agonda Beach offers a peaceful retreat. This pristine beach is less crowded, making it an ideal spot for naturists who prefer solitude. The gentle waves and expansive sandy shores provide a perfect backdrop for quiet reflection or leisurely walks. The surrounding village is quaint and welcoming, offering a glimpse into the simple, laid-back lifestyle of the locals.

Palolem Beach, with its crescent shape and calm waters, is another popular choice. While not traditionally a naturist destination, certain sections of the beach are known to be more tolerant of naturist practices. The relaxed atmosphere, combined with the natural beauty, makes Palolem a perfect spot for both relaxation and exploration. The beach is also known for its vibrant nightlife and eclectic dining options, adding to its charm.

Whether you're a seasoned naturist or new to the experience, Goa's open beaches offer a liberating escape. The chance to connect with nature, explore diverse cultures, and recharge your spirit is unparalleled. As you plan your visit, be sure to research and respect local guidelines to ensure a harmonious experience. Embrace the freedom and beauty that these stunning beaches have to offer—your journey to a revitalized self awaits.

In conclusion, Goa's open beaches provide an idyllic setting for naturists, blending natural beauty with cultural richness. Whether you seek the vibrant energy of Arambol and Anjuna or the peaceful retreat of Agonda and Palolem, these beaches promise a memorable and rejuvenating experience. Embrace the freedom, respect the culture, and immerse yourself in the stunning landscapes that make Goa a naturist paradise.

As you leave the shores of Goa, the memories of sunlit days and starry nights will linger. The warmth of the sun, the rhythm of the waves, and the sense of community will stay with you, inspiring future adventures and a continued appreciation for the naturist lifestyle. Goa's open beaches are not just a destination—they are a celebration of freedom, nature, and the joy of living fully.

Kerala Backwaters – A phenomenal network of lagoons, lakes, canals, and rivers, the Kerala Backwaters promise an experience that's as serene as it is captivating. Known for their picturesque beauty and tranquil surroundings, these backwaters offer naturists an unparalleled opportunity to immerse themselves in nature unclad, and in harmony with the rhythms of life that flow through this aquatic paradise.

When one first embarks on a houseboat journey through Kerala's vast labyrinth of waterways, it becomes clear that this is a special place. Sunlight dances on the gently rippling water, casting golden reflections on the lush, sprawling palm groves that line the canals. This undisturbed nature strongly resonates with the core principles of naturism – simplicity, freedom, and connection with the environment. For those seeking a more liberating and intimate experience, the Kerala Backwaters offer pockets of seclusion where naturism can be embraced without inhibition, merging the physical freedom of nudity with the mental tranquility of the natural setting.

Imagine floating lazily down the water, secluded from the world, surrounded by the calls of exotic birds and the rustling of palm trees. Kerala's unique ecosystem supports a diverse array of wildlife, making it an ideal spot for birdwatchers and nature lovers alike. Kingfishers, darters, terns, and cormorants skim the water's surface, while bulbuls, woodpeckers, and parrots animate the verdant backdrop of the shores. Observing these creatures in their natural habitats, with nothing but the breath of the backwaters against your skin, enhances the feeling of oneness with nature that is central to the naturist ethos.

The houseboats themselves, traditional 'kettuvallams', are masterpieces of craftsmanship. Constructed from local materials like bamboo poles, coconut fiber ropes, and teak wood, these floating retreats provide all modern comforts while harmonizing with the surroundings. Relaxing in the comfort of these houseboats, naturist travelers can gaze at the endless horizon, undeterred by the presence of textiles. It's this blend of luxury and freedom that makes the Kerala Backwaters a standout destination for those dedicated to naturist travel.

Time slows down here – and that's an integral part of the experience. The backwaters are a place of reflection and relaxation, providing the perfect backdrop for naturist yoga and meditation. Imagine doing sun salutations on the deck at dawn, surrounded by the morning mist, or meditating to the gentle soundscape created by the ripples and bird songs. Such activities not only enhance your physical well-being but also deepen your spiritual connection to this serene environment.

While the backwaters offer remoteness, they are by no means isolated from the rich culture and heritage of Kerala. The local communities living along the banks have thrived here for centuries, developing a symbiotic relationship with the waters. As your boat glides past small villages and vibrant paddy fields, you'll witness the daily lives of the Kerala people – fishermen casting their nets, women washing clothes, and children waving joyously. This cultural interweaving enriches the naturist experience, reminding us that naturism isn't about escape but about being an integral part of the ecosystem.

Engaging with the local culture can lead to an even more profound appreciation of the backwaters. Cooking classes on board, for example, offer a chance to learn the secrets of Kerala's famous cuisine, utilizing fresh and local ingredients. Sampling freshly prepared meals, rich in coconut and spices, while embodying the simple and natural lifestyle of naturism, creates a holistic travel experience that nourishes both body and soul.

The Kerala Backwaters are also known for their Ayurvedic treatments. Dotted along the winding waterways are wellness retreats where you can indulge in rejuvenating therapies. Ayurveda, the traditional Indian system of medicine, is based on balancing the body's Vata, Pitta, and Kapha doshas (energetic forces of nature) through diet, herbal treatments, and lifestyle choices. Receiving an Ayurvedic massage or participating in a cleanse, unencumbered by clothing, can enhance the healing process, amplifying the rejuvenating effects of both naturism and Ayurveda.

Of course, naturists must remain mindful of local customs and ensure that their practices do not offend or disrupt the prevailing social norms. While the backwaters provide secluded spots ideal for naturism, it's essential to navigate this space with respect and sensitivity, engaging with local guides who understand the balance between freedom and cultural acknowledgment. Opting for private houseboat charters ensures that your naturist practices remain harmonious with the surroundings.

When the day reaches its end, nothing compares to the backwaters at twilight. The sky transforms into a canvas, painted with hues of orange, pink, and purple, mirroring itself upon the still waters. This symphony of color is a magical sight, best enjoyed while drifting through the tranquil waterways, free from the burdens of clothing and worldly concerns. As darkness settles, the gentle sounds of nocturnal creatures begin their chorus, serenading you to sleep under the Kerala stars.

In sum, the Kerala Backwaters offer a sanctum where naturists can experience unparalleled natural beauty and tranquility. It's a place to disconnect from the chaos of modern life and reconnect with the essence of nature, all while living in harmony with an ancient culture. Whether you're practicing yoga on a houseboat deck at sunrise, soaking in the lush scenery from a famous 'kettuvallam', or savoring the serene symphony of the backwaters at dusk, Kerala's aquatic paradise unfurls as a truly liberating and unforgettable naturist destination.

Chapter 12:
Oceania's Naturist Delights

Oceania offers some of the most liberating and picturesque naturist experiences, making it a haven for those seeking to embrace the freedom of nudity amidst nature's beauty. In Australia, the vast expanses of the Outback seamlessly blend into idyllic beaches, such as those around Sydney and the sprawling, sun-kissed shores of Queensland. Each spot invites naturists to shed their layers and immerse themselves in pure natural splendor. Across the Tasman Sea, New Zealand hosts its own gems, providing a backdrop of dramatic landscapes where one can feel naturally free. From the lush forests to serene coastal hideaways, the Land of the Long White Cloud promises an unparalleled and rejuvenating naturist retreat. Embrace the ultimate expression of freedom in these lands where the sky meets the sea, and every moment feels like a harmonious dance with nature itself.

Australia: Bare Down Under

As you explore Oceania's naturist offerings, you'll find that Australia holds its own special allure for naturists seeking both adventure and tranquility. Imagine pristine beaches stretching as far as the eye can see, with the golden sands of the Queensland coasts beckoning you to shed your clothes and your worries. From the secluded spots around Sydney, where the blue waters sparkle under the sun, to the wildly beautiful terrains that encourage you to reconnect with nature in its most authentic form, Australia is a paradise for those who embrace the naturist lifestyle. Whether you're taking a refreshing dip in the ocean or basking in the warm sunlight, Australia's naturist spots provide an unmatchable blend of freedom and natural beauty, inviting you to experience the continent's unique charm, free from the confines of clothing.

Sydney Surroundings offers an enchanting array of naturist experiences, making it an essential stop for those exploring Oceania's naturist delights. Known not just for its iconic Opera House and Harbour Bridge, Sydney reveals a subtler charm in its proximate naturist spots that promise both tranquility and adventure.

The leafy outskirts of Sydney play host to a spectrum of naturist-friendly environments. One can't miss discovering the liberating essence of Cobblers Beach, tucked neatly within the serene bushlands of Middle Head. Its inviting stretch of golden sand and crystal-clear waters make it a haven for sunbathing and swimming in the nude. The beach, known for its secluded ambience, draws a mixed crowd of both locals and travelers seeking a genuine naturist experience free of crowds and commercialization. Spend a day here, and it becomes clear why many call it a naturist's paradise.

A short drive from the city center leads to the picturesque Lady Bay Beach. This petite beach, located in the affluent suburb of Watsons Bay, is a hallmark of naturist tradition in Sydney. Originally proclaimed a nude bathing area in 1976, Lady Bay Beach remains a testament to the region's progressive stance on naturism. Visitors often find themselves mesmerized by the stunning harbor views, the gentle lapping of waves against the pebbled shore, and the leafy cliffs that cocoon the beach in privacy and natural beauty.

For those who seek a blend of naturism within a social and supportive community, the local naturist clubs around Sydney offer a warm welcome. The Sun Club, one of Australia's oldest naturist clubs, provides a sanctuary for social nudity enthusiasts. Located amidst the lushness of Camperdown, the club hosts numerous events and gatherings that allow newcomers and seasoned naturists to mingle, share stories, and participate in activities from barbecues to yoga sessions. The Sun Club is perfect for connecting with like-minded individuals in a safe, judgment-free environment.

Equally enticing is the Twin Rivers Clothing Optional Resort. Nestled in the verdant landscapes of Kangaroo Valley, this resort is a couple of hours' drive from Sydney and offers a more secluded and rustic naturist experience. With facilities that range from cozy cabins to campsites by the river, Twin Rivers promises a retreat into nature. It's an ideal spot for those looking to unwind under the stars, enjoy peaceful swims in the river, or explore the nearby trails and waterfalls in their natural state.

No exploration of Sydney's naturist surroundings would be complete without mentioning River Island Nature Retreat. Situated in the rolling hills near the Burragorang Valley, this expansive retreat has gained a reputation for its picturesque camping sites, lush greenery, and the flowing river that gently curves through the property. Activities here are tailored to maximize the naturist experience, whether it's hiking naked through the expansive property, basking in the sun on the riverbank, or participating in community-organized events. River Island offers an unpretentious, nature-immersed escape that captivates the spirit.

Sydney's moderate climate adds to its allure, providing almost year-round opportunities for naturist activities. The temperate weather ensures that outdoor adventures remain pleasant, whether you're trekking through coastal trails, lounging on a beach, or picnicking in a naturist park. The region's biodiversity, with its array of native flora and fauna, enhances the sensory experience, grounding you in the natural world and heightening the feeling of liberation.

Throughout your time exploring Sydney's naturist hotspots, keep in mind the accepted etiquette in these places. Respect and consideration for fellow naturists, as well as an understanding of the local rules and guidelines, ensure a harmonious and enjoyable experience for everyone. Engaging with the environment respectfully, leaving no trace, and interacting with both wildlife and fellow visitors with kindness and sensitivity are paramount practices that uphold the naturist principles.

Don't miss out on the unique opportunity to sample local cuisine in naturist-friendly settings within the city's surroundings. Several venues, like those in the Blue Mountains area, offer naturist dining experiences where you can savor Australia's culinary delights in a liberating environment. Imagine enjoying a freshly prepared meal with views of rolling hills and valleys, your body free of the constraints of clothing and your senses fully attuned to the pleasures of taste and nature.

The Sydney surroundings, with their composite mix of beaches, communities, and retreats, make up a tapestry of naturist experiences that are as varied as they are exhilarating. Whether seeking solitude on a pristine beach or camaraderie within a welcoming club, naturists can find their niche amid Sydney's diverse offerings. So, let Sydney be a part of your naturist journey, a place where the urban and the natural come together to create a haven of freedom and exploration. This chapter of your travels will undoubtedly add a rich, unforgettable contour to your global naturist adventure.

Queensland Coasts Nestled in the northeastern corner of Australia, Queensland boasts some of the world's most idyllic coastlines, perfect for naturist adventures. With its warm, tropical climate and a backdrop of lush rainforests, this region offers a unique blend of natural beauty and liberating experiences. From the bustling beaches near Brisbane to the secluded shores of the Whitsunday Islands, Queensland's coasts are a naturist's delight.

The Sunshine Coast, located just north of Brisbane, is renowned for its expansive, golden beaches and azure waters. One of the prime naturist spots here is Alexandria Bay, affectionately known as "A-Bay." It's a bit of a trek to get there, but the journey through Noosa National Park only adds to the experience. As you navigate this picturesque trail, fringed by coastal banksias and pandanus trees, the anticipation builds. When you finally set foot on the powdery sands of A-Bay, the reward is a serene, clothing-optional beach that feels like a hidden sanctuary.

Further north, the elongated stretch of sand along the Fraser Coast beckons. Of particular interest to naturists is Inskip Point, near Rainbow Beach. This scenic location offers a more rugged, untouched ambiance. With dunes rising on one side and the vast Pacific on the other, it's an ideal spot for those seeking solitude. The campgrounds here are popular with naturists, providing a perfect base from which to explore the coast in your natural state. Waking up to the sound of waves crashing and stepping out into the fresh morning air, free of clothing, is a liberating start to any day.

Traversing even further north, the Whitsunday Islands emerge as a tropical paradise par excellence. These islands, dotted across the Coral Sea, are famed for their pristine beaches and clear waters. Whitehaven Beach, in particular, is a must-visit. Though it isn't officially recognized as a naturist beach, its remote beauty and expansive space often make it an unofficial hotspot for those wanting to shed their shackles. Imagine sailing through turquoise waters, anchoring your boat, and stepping onto the pristine white silica sand, letting the sun embrace every inch of your skin. It's an unforgettable experience, with breathtaking views at every turn.

For those venturing to the northern reaches of Queensland, the Cairns and Port Douglas area offers many hidden gems. Nudey Beach, located on Fitzroy Island, is particularly noteworthy. Despite its playful name, it's a favorite among naturists for its intimacy and beauty. The beach can be reached by a short but scenic hike through lush forest, which opens up to reveal a tranquil cove perfect for swimming and sunbathing in the nude. It's a peaceful retreat from the more tourist-heavy spots and ensures a deep connection with nature.

The sense of freedom that pervades Queensland's beaches extends beyond just nudity. There's a genuine feeling of being at one with nature. The Great Barrier Reef, which lies just offshore, adds an extra layer of wonder to the experience. Snorkeling or diving in these waters allows naturists to explore a vibrant underwater world, teeming with coral and marine life, enhancing the sense of adventure.

Practical considerations are also crucial for a successful naturist trip. Understanding local customs and respecting other beachgoers is essential. While many of these beaches are unofficially clothing-optional, it's always a good idea to check local guidelines and be mindful of others. Also, sun protection is paramount. The Queensland sun can be intense, and without clothing, you're more exposed. Eco-friendly sunscreens are highly recommended to protect both your skin and the delicate marine environments.

If you're planning an extended stay, Queensland offers various naturist-friendly accommodations. From secluded beachside rentals to naturist resorts, there's a range of options to suit different preferences. Some resorts even provide organized activities such as yoga, meditation, and social events, allowing naturists to connect with like-minded individuals and enhance their journey.

The Queensland coasts are not just about sun and sand; they offer a deeper, more holistic connection to nature. Whether you're hiking to a secluded beach, sailing among islands, or simply enjoying the sun on your skin, this region has a special magic that resonates deeply with naturists. Each beach, each shore has its own charm and provides a unique experience, making Queensland a top destination for naturist travel.

Ultimately, the freedom and beauty found along Queensland's coasts provide an unparalleled naturist experience. As you walk these sun-kissed beaches, the rhythmic song of the ocean in your ears, you may find a sense of liberation that goes beyond just the absence of clothing. It's an embrace of the natural world, a dance with the elements, and a truly enriching adventure for the soul.

New Zealand: Naturally Free

New Zealand, known for its breathtaking landscapes and welcoming culture, is a naturist's dream. This remote Pacific paradise offers countless opportunities for those seeking an unadulterated connection with nature. Whether you're wandering through verdant forests, basking on pristine beaches, or soaking in hot springs, New Zealand provides the perfect backdrop for naturism.

Nestled in the southwestern Pacific Ocean, New Zealand consists of two main landmasses—the North and South Islands—and around 600 smaller islands. Each region has its unique charm and offers distinct naturist experiences. On the North Island, the mild climate and extensive shoreline make it a haven for beach lovers. You can find secluded, sandy stretches where you can strip down and soak up the sun without a care in the world.

The South Island, with its rugged terrains and striking fjords, caters to those seeking adventure in their naturist pursuits. Here, you can embark on challenging hikes that reward you with panoramic views and hidden spots perfect for a solitary, clothes-free moment. The diversity of landscapes means that no matter your preference, New Zealand has something to offer.

One standout destination in the North Island is Waihi Beach. Known for its long, golden sands and clear blue waters, this beach is a favorite among naturists. The southern end, particularly, is renowned for being quieter and more remote, offering the privacy naturists cherish. Don't be surprised if you find yourself completely alone, embraced by nature's raw beauty.

Further south, you'll discover the Coromandel Peninsula, another naturist hotspot. Its secluded bays and lush, green hills present multiple options for naturist exploration. Otama Beach, with its soft sands and unspoiled environment, is a must-visit. This beach, often empty during weekdays, provides the ideal setting for a relaxing, clothes-free afternoon.

Moving to the South Island, the Abel Tasman National Park is an extraordinary place for any naturist. The park's coastal track winds through some of the country's most stunning scenery—golden beaches, turquoise waters, and dense, native forests. Naturism is well-received here, as long as one respects the park's guidelines and other visitors. The tranquility of this location will let you immerse yourself in nature, experiencing a profound sense of freedom.

For a more adventurous naturist, tackling the paths of Arthur's Pass National Park is essential. This alpine dominion is characterized by jagged mountains, deep gorges, and breathtaking waterfalls. While the terrain may be demanding, the promise of finding isolated spots where you can unwind nude amidst nature's grandeur makes it worthwhile.

In New Zealand, even urban areas support the naturist lifestyle. Wellington, the country's vibrant capital, is home to Breaker Bay, a legally recognized nude beach. This urban escape allows you to enjoy naturist freedom without venturing far from city amenities. The beach is conveniently close to the city center but feels like a hidden gem, with rocks and rugged coastline creating natural enclosures.

Naturistically-inclined visitors to Auckland can venture to Little Palm Beach on Waiheke Island. Just a short ferry ride from the bustling city, this beach's serene ambiance offers a comforting sense of privacy. As you shed your clothes and worries, you may realize how uniquely harmonious naturism and urbanity can be in New Zealand.

New Zealand also promotes social naturism through well-established clubs. Auckland Outdoor Naturist Club and Wellington Naturist Club provide safe and welcoming environments for new and seasoned naturists alike. These clubs are fantastic ways to socialized with like-minded individuals and get insider tips on the best naturist spots in the country. They often organize events that deepen your connection to the community and allow you to explore New Zealand's naturist facets more extensively.

Moving away from the beaches and into geothermal territories, Rotorua on the North Island offers another unique naturist experience. Known for its hot springs and geysers, Rotorua invites you to bathe as nature intended. Kuirau Park's natural hot pools provide an open-air opportunity to relax in the therapeutic waters. The surroundings—emerald foliage, steaming vents, and bubbling mud pools—create an otherworldly atmosphere that enhances the naturist experience.

For those looking for an entirely naturist retreat, Tui Naturist Park near Nelson on the South Island is an ideal spot. Surrounded by woodland and native bush, this park provides a tranquil setting for a naturist holiday. With its combination of private cabins and open camping areas, Tui Naturist Park caters to various preferences. The environment is all about relaxation and letting go of societal constraints, fostering a stronger connection to nature.

One cannot discuss New Zealand without mentioning its affinity for outdoor sports. Activities such as kayaking, horseback riding, and even bungee jumping are available for the daring naturist. Imagine the exhilaration of kayaking through the calm waters of the Marlborough Sounds with nothing but sunscreen between you and nature. It's an electrifying way to experience natural freedom.

Whichever adventure you choose, New Zealand's emphasis on respecting nature aligns perfectly with naturist principles. Without the barriers of clothing, you'll find a truer appreciation for the environment around you. Each flower, each rock, each wave of the ocean takes on a new significance when experienced in the full embrace of nature.

In addition to natural and recreational opportunities, New Zealand's culture plays a supportive role in making this a top naturist destination. The Māori concept of "Kaitiakitanga" denotes guardianship and protection over the land, sea, and sky. This respect for nature translates into a sensible, welcoming attitude towards naturism. As you travel through New Zealand, you'll find that this cultural backbone fosters a community spirit and acceptance of different ways of living.

As with any naturist destination, it's crucial to stay informed about local guidelines and etiquette. New Zealand's general lenience towards public nudity does not supersede the need for respectful behavior. Make sure you're in an area that welcomes naturism and always practice the principles of "leave no trace."

New Zealand stands out as one of the most naturally suited places for naturism. From its awe-inspiring landscapes to its open-hearted culture, it provides a sanctuary for anyone looking to reconnect with themselves and the world around them. Embrace this island nation's vast array of naturist possibilities, and you'll likely find that you've encountered the very essence of being "naturally free."

Chapter 13:
Travel Tips for Naturist Tours

Embarking on a naturist tour is an exhilarating experience that calls for some essential preparation to ensure an uninterrupted, delightful journey. Begin by securing accommodations that openly embrace naturism, as this will allow you to be in a relaxed and accepting environment from the get-go. Platforms dedicated to naturist travel often list such destinations, making your search much easier. When traveling to countries where English isn't widely spoken, consider learning basic phrases in the local language. This can greatly enhance interactions and demonstrates respect for the local culture. Additionally, carrying a lightweight sarong or wrap can be invaluable, offering flexibility and convenience when transitioning between naturist and textile areas. By planning ahead and staying considerate of both legal and cultural nuances, you'll savor the freedom and joy that come with a naturist adventure.

Finding Naturist-friendly Accommodations

Finding the perfect naturist-friendly accommodation can often make or break your travel experience. Whether you're seeking a luxurious resort or a charming bed and breakfast, knowing where to look and what to expect can lead to an unforgettable stay. So let's navigate through the myriad options that promise both comfort and a welcoming, naturist-friendly atmosphere.

Firstly, researching your destination heavily impacts your accommodation choice. Naturist accommodations come in various forms—ranging from sprawling resorts to homey guesthouses. Websites dedicated to naturist travel, as well as community forums, can be valuable resources. Reading reviews on platforms like TripAdvisor alongside naturist-specific sites helps gauge the vibe, cleanliness, and authenticity.

When it comes to luxury, naturist resorts stand out. These resorts often provide not only accommodation but also activities and amenities designed specifically for naturists. For instance, Cap d'Agde in France offers a broad range of luxury options, from villas with private pools to beachfront bungalows. Similar grandeur can be found in places like Hidden Beach Resort in Mexico, which boast top-notch services while promoting a naturist-friendly environment.

While luxury resorts are certainly enticing, don't overlook the charm of smaller, boutique-style guesthouses and bed-and-breakfasts. These accommodations often offer a more personal experience, fostering a close-knit community feel. In places like the Canary Islands and Greece, you'll find numerous family-run establishments that welcome naturists with open arms. Many of these spots cultivate an ambiance that's both intimate and inclusive.

The idea of camping may not immediately spring to mind, yet naturist camping sites are a fantastic option for those who love the great outdoors. Naturist campsites are often more affordable and provide immersive experiences in nature. In destinations like Croatia's nudist camps or the naturist campgrounds in British Columbia, you can pitch your tent within serene, forested surroundings or right by the dazzling waters. Additionally, many of these sites offer facilities such as communal kitchens, showers, and common areas where like-minded travelers can socialize.

Vacation rentals also present a flexible option for naturist accommodations. Websites like Airbnb and Vrbo have filters allowing you to find properties that accommodate naturist lifestyles. Renting a private apartment or house means you get the freedom to tailor your stay exactly how you wish, often with added privacy. This can be especially appealing if you're new to naturism and still growing comfortable with the lifestyle.

Understanding the cultural context of your travel destination is paramount when choosing accommodation. In some countries, naturism is more widely accepted and integrated into the local way of life, making it easier to find suitable lodging. For instance, naturist accommodations in the Netherlands or the liberal beaches of Spain are abundant and straightforward to book. However, in regions where naturism is less common or more restricted, the choices might be fewer and should be selected with extra care.

Another critical consideration is the amenities and services offered by your chosen accommodation. Check if the place provides naturist-friendly pools, beaches, or common areas. Some accommodations offer wellness services tailored for naturists like yoga and meditation classes, saunas, and guided nature walks. These can substantially enrich your stay, providing relaxation and an opportunity to connect deeper with the naturist community.

Don't forget, the community aspect of naturist accommodation is vital. Naturist resorts and hotels often host events and activities encouraging social interactions among guests. Whether it's a communal dinner, a beach volleyball game, or a group excursion, these activities help foster friendships and community bonds. Many travelers find these social aspects incredibly enriching, adding a distinct layer to their traveling experience.

Finding the right naturist-friendly accommodation also involves some logistical planning. Always confirm the specifics before booking—like whether the entire property is naturist or just certain areas, and if there are rules about dress codes. This prevents any misunderstandings and ensures your expectations align with what's offered. Additionally, make sure to check the size of the establishment and the level of privacy provided, especially if you're looking for a quieter experience.

As you embark on your search, it's invaluable to join naturist travel forums and social media groups. Here, you'll find honest reviews and recommendations from fellow naturist travelers. These communities often highlight lesser-known gems, providing insights you might not come across in conventional travel research. Furthermore, connecting with seasoned naturist travelers can equip you with tips and experiences that enrich your own journey.

One should not overlook the potential benefits of travel agents who specialize in naturist travel. They can tailor your trip to your specific desires, handle bookings, and provide expert advice on the best destinations and accommodations suited for naturists. Such specialized services can significantly ease the process, freeing you from the hassle and ensuring your vacation is seamless and enjoyable.

Safety is another critical factor. Always ensure that the naturist-friendly accommodation upholds high safety and security standards. Reading through detailed reviews and checking for accreditation can provide peace of mind. Safety features like secure locks, adequate lighting, and respectful, professional staff play crucial roles in fostering a comfortable environment.

Lastly, always keep an open mind and a sense of adventure. While high-end resorts offer comfort and luxury, sometimes the most memorable experiences come from unexpected places. Maybe it's a tiny, off-the-grid naturist campsite in Uruguay or an unexpected, welcoming guest house in the heart of Tuscany. Embrace the diversity of accommodations available and enjoy the unique flavors each brings to your naturist travel experience.

Finding naturist-friendly accommodations is an exciting part of planning your travel. With thoughtful research, clear expectations, and an adventurous spirit, you're sure to find the perfect spot that guarantees both comfort and a liberating naturist atmosphere. Happy travels!

Navigating Language Barriers

Traveling to a new country, especially on a naturist tour, offers both exhilarating freedom and the potential challenge of navigating language barriers. While naturism promotes a universal language of body positivity and acceptance, practical communication remains essential. Here's how to ensure language differences don't mar your liberating experience.

First and foremost, learning a few basic phrases in the local language can make a world of difference. A simple "hello," "thank you," or "please" can open doors and hearts. It's not just about words, though; it's about showing respect for the culture you're visiting. An effort to speak the local language often garners appreciation and smoother interactions.

Consider carrying a pocket dictionary or a translation app on your smartphone. Modern technology has brought us numerous tools, such as Google Translate or iTranslate, which can translate spoken and written language in real-time. These apps are particularly handy for reading menus, signs, or communicating with locals who may not speak English.

However, technology might not replace the warmth of human interaction. Don't underestimate the power of body language, facial expressions, and gestures. A friendly smile, a nod, or open hand movements can convey respect and a willingness to connect, transcending linguistic boundaries.

When choosing a naturist destination, it's often beneficial to book accommodations or tours through agencies that specialize in naturist travel. These agencies typically employ staff who are fluent in multiple languages and familiar with the unique needs of naturist travelers. This additional layer of support can alleviate potential communication challenges, especially in remote regions.

In some countries, the naturist community itself may act as a bridge. Many naturist venues, resorts, and beaches have an international clientele, and it's common to find fellow travelers. Engaging in conversation with other naturists can provide invaluable tips, local knowledge, and even help with interpretations.

If you're joining an organized naturist event or festival, make sure to inform the organizers about your language preferences in advance. Many international events offer multilingual assistance, whether through staff, informational pamphlets, or programmed tours. Knowing there's language support can make you feel more at ease, allowing you to immerse yourself fully in the experience.

Furthermore, consider immersing yourself in visual aids. Maps, diagrams, and pictograms frequently break through language barriers. Many naturist resorts and facilities utilize universally recognized symbols to denote areas like dining spaces, restrooms, and recreational zones. Familiarizing yourself with these symbols beforehand can enhance your self-reliance in unfamiliar environments.

For those looking to explore naturist destinations in more remote or less tourist-heavy regions, hiring a local guide might be a wise investment. A knowledgeable guide not only bridges the language gap but also offers cultural insights and access to off-the-beaten-path spots.

Their presence can also make navigating legalities and social norms easier, particularly in places where naturism is less common.

Planning your trip with cultural and language research can be invaluable. Before departure, delve into travel guides, blogs, and videos about your destination. Forums and social media groups dedicated to naturist travel are treasure troves of collective wisdom and personal anecdotes. Oftentimes, seasoned naturists share their experiences with language barriers, offering practical tips and reassurance.

While on your journey, stay adaptable and patient. Misunderstandings are bound to happen, but approaching situations with a calm and open-minded attitude can turn potential frustrations into memorable experiences. It's all part of the adventure and growth that come with travel.

Lastly, remember that naturism itself can act as a universal language. The shared value of body acceptance and the communal spirit of naturist environments often create an atmosphere where communication flows more freely. In settings where everyone embraces simplicity and authenticity, the need for spoken words sometimes diminishes, making space for genuine human connection beyond linguistic constraints.

By implementing these strategies, you'll find that navigating language barriers can enhance your naturist travel experience, turning potential obstacles into opportunities for deeper connections and richer experiences in the beautiful, liberating naturist spots around the world.

Chapter 14:
Embracing Naturism Within Different Cultures

Navigating the world of naturism requires a deep understanding and respect for the diverse cultures you'll encounter on your travels. Each destination carries its unique set of customs and attitudes towards nudity, making it crucial for naturists to approach with a mindful and open heart. Imagine strolling on a secluded beach in Greece, feeling the ancient spirit of freedom, or participating in a local festival in Brazil where the body is celebrated in its natural form. These experiences not only offer a tactile connection to the land but also foster a greater appreciation for the local traditions and mores. Recognizing and embracing these cultural differences enrich your journey, ensuring that every naturist adventure is not just a holiday but a harmonious blend of exploration and respect.

Respectful Travel Practices

When you're venturing into the naturist lifestyle, respecting local customs and practices is non-negotiable. You'll find that embracing and adhering to respectful travel practices not only enhances your experience but also ensures that naturist destinations remain accepted and open for future visitors.

One of the fundamental principles to keep in mind is to always respect the culture and norms of the country or region you're visiting. Naturism, even though it's about freedom and being in tune with nature, can be perceived very differently around the world. For instance, what might be perfectly acceptable on a Caribbean beach could be looked upon with disapproval in many parts of Asia. Awareness of these cultural nuances is essential. Research or ask locals about the norms to avoid misunderstandings.

Communication is key. Often, language barriers can lead to misunderstandings, but a friendly demeanor and a willingness to adhere to local customs can bridge this gap. Learn basic phrases, greetings, and perhaps even a bit of etiquette in the local language. Showing that you're making an effort to understand and respect the culture goes a long way. It doesn't just smooth your travel experience; it fosters goodwill and better interactions.

Additionally, be mindful of where and when it's appropriate to be nude. Public nudity laws vary greatly around the world, and enforcement can be strict. Even in countries with established naturist resorts or beaches, being nude in non-designated areas can cause problems. Always keep an eye out for signs or guidelines, and if you're unsure, consult local naturist organizations or forums. They are often the best sources for up-to-date and accurate information on local practices.

Respectful behavior extends beyond your attire. Your demeanor and actions should be considerate too. This means not taking photos of others without consent, respecting personal space, and refraining from overtly sexual behavior, which is generally discouraged in naturist environments. Naturism is about freedom and acceptance, and maintaining this positive atmosphere requires genuine respect and mindfulness from everyone involved.

Respecting local privacy is another crucial aspect. In some places, locals may be comfortable with naturism within private resorts but not in public view. Understanding and honoring these boundaries prevents discomfort and fosters positive relationships between visitors and local communities.

Respect for the environment can't be overstated. Naturists often choose this lifestyle to be closer to nature, so it's vital to practice environmental stewardship. This means adhering to 'leave no trace' principles: picking up after yourself, minimizing waste, and being conscientious of wildlife and natural habitats. Preserving the natural beauty of these places is not just about your visit, but ensuring that future generations can enjoy them too.

Visibility and advocacy of respectful practices can also have a ripple effect. Take the opportunity to gently educate fellow travelers about the importance of these practices. Whether through conversations or social media posts, you can highlight the positive impact of respectful naturism. This not only promotes responsible travel but also contributes to a broader public understanding and acceptance of naturism.

Often, communities near naturist spots may have mixed feelings about naturism. Engage respectfully with locals, shop at local businesses, and be a good ambassador for the naturist lifestyle. Positive interactions can help dispel myths and build a supportive atmosphere for naturism. Many destinations rely heavily on tourism, and showing that naturists respect and contribute to the local economy can bolster acceptance.

Respect for other travelers is just as important. Naturist destinations attract people from various walks of life, and everyone's comfort level with nudity can vary. If someone seems unsure or uncomfortable, be approachable and open without being intrusive. Help create an atmosphere of acceptance and respect, ensuring that everyone can enjoy the experience at their own pace.

Naturism in diverse cultures also means being flexible and non-judgmental. What naturism looks like can vary widely; in some cultures, it may be more about tranquility and solitude, while in others, it might involve socializing and festivals. Embrace these differences – they're part of what makes your travel experience rich and fulfilling.

Being discreet with naturism-related discussions in conservative or non-naturist areas is also wise. Not every place will be open or accepting of naturism, and loudly discussing your naturist plans in a traditional setting could be seen as disrespectful. Save those conversations for more private moments or designated naturist areas where they're more appropriate.

Lastly, your journey as a respectful naturist traveler might well influence how the local community evolves. By setting a positive example, you can help foster an environment where naturism is increasingly understood, respected, and integrated. This not only enriches your experience but also ensures that naturist travel can continue to thrive.

Adhering to respectful travel practices is more than just following rules; it's about embodying the core principles of naturism: respect for oneself, others, and the environment. In doing so, you contribute positively to a global community of naturists, ensuring that these beautiful destinations remain cherished places of freedom and unity. So, embark on your naturist adventures with a spirit of respect and openness, and you'll find the world's beauty not just in its landscapes, but in its diverse cultures too.

Cultural Sensitivities and Awareness

When embracing naturism in different cultures, understanding and respecting cultural sensitivities becomes paramount. Every society holds unique views and customs related to nudity, stemming from historical, religious, and social contexts. As travelers, it is crucial to approach these cultural landscapes with an open mind and a respectful demeanor. This section will delve into how one can navigate through diverse cultural terrains while engaging in naturist activities.

To begin with, it is important to remember that nudity represents various things to different people. In some cultures, nudity is seen as a return to naturalism and purity, while in others, it could be considered taboo or offensive. In Western Europe, for instance, naturism is widely accepted and even celebrated in places like France and Spain. The beaches are often dotted with naturist-friendly signs, and the locals usually embrace the lifestyle. However, one must still be aware of regional variances; what is acceptable in the Canary Islands might not be as easily accepted in more conservative inland areas.

In contrast, parts of Asia present a more complex scenario. Thailand, for example, has seen a growing acceptance of naturism, yet the cultural nuances related to modesty remain deeply entrenched. Thai society highly values decorum and respect, particularly concerning religious sites and public spaces. Therefore, understanding the boundaries and specific areas designated for naturism is essential to avoid unintended offense.

Moving on to the Middle East, naturism is often considered at odds with societal norms, grounded in deep-rooted religious and cultural values that prioritize modesty. Israel offers a few secluded beaches where naturism can be enjoyed discreetly, but travelers should remain conscious of the conservative ethos prevalent in broader society. Knowledge about local customs, such as attire and public behavior, will certainly go a long way in ensuring respectful interactions.

Educating oneself about local laws and regulations is another critical aspect. Legal frameworks surrounding naturism vary widely around the globe. In places like Croatia, the law may be more lenient in designated areas, while in some countries, public nudity could invite legal repercussions. Research and preparation are necessary to avoid any legal troubles. Organizations and local naturist groups often provide valuable insights and recommendations, making them a good resource for travelers.

Furthermore, cultivating an attitude of empathy and open-mindedness can significantly enhance your naturist adventures. By engaging with locals and understanding their perspectives, you not only gain a deeper appreciation for the culture but also pave the way for meaningful connections. A respectful approach can often open doors to hidden naturist spots known only to the local community.

Communication barriers can also pose challenges. Learning basic phrases in the local language, such as polite greetings and expressions of gratitude, can make a world of difference. In regions where naturism is less understood, being able to explain your intentions clearly and respectfully can alleviate potential misunderstandings. Language can act as a bridge, fostering mutual respect and awareness.

One effective strategy for culturally sensitive naturist travel is to seek out and participate in organized naturist activities and events. These activities are typically well-structured and adhere to local guidelines, offering a secure environment to enjoy naturism. Festivals, retreats, and guided tours often provide the dual benefit of cultural immersion and naturist experience, ensuring that both aspects are harmoniously integrated.

In addition, respecting the privacy and preferences of fellow naturists and locals is essential. Always ask for consent before taking photos, and be mindful of shared spaces. What might be a casual photograph for you could be a breach of privacy for someone else, especially in more conservative settings. Such practices foster a considerate and inclusive environment, ensuring that naturism remains a liberating experience for everyone involved.

As naturism increasingly intersects with global travel, adopting a mindset of cultural sensitivity and awareness has never been more crucial. While the allure of experiencing naturism amidst breathtaking landscapes might be the key motivation, the journey should always be underscored by respect and understanding. Each destination offers its unique blend of beauty, culture, and tradition; by approaching each with curiosity and sensitivity, travelers can truly enrich their naturist experiences.

To sum up, embracing naturism within different cultures is an enriching yet delicate endeavor. It demands an appreciation for diversity and a keen awareness of local customs and laws. By preparing thoroughly, engaging respectfully, and maintaining an open heart and mind, naturist travelers can enjoy a fulfilling and harmonious journey across the globe. Always remember, the essence of naturism is not just the physical freedom it affords but also the shared human experience that transcends cultural boundaries.

Chapter 15:
Sustainable and Ethical Naturist Travel

As our journeys lead us to untouched naturist paradises, it's crucial to navigate with a light footprint and a heart rooted in respect. Embracing sustainable and ethical naturist travel means making environmentally conscious decisions, like opting for eco-friendly accommodations and reducing waste, thereby preserving these natural havens for future explorers. Supporting local communities is equally vital; by engaging with local artisans and businesses, we ensure that our travels contribute positively to the places we cherish. This harmonious blend of mindful practices not only enriches your own experience but also fosters a deeper connection with the land and its people, crafting a more profound and meaningful adventure.

Environmentally Conscious Choices

Making thoughtful, environmentally conscious choices isn't just about preserving the beauty of our naturist destinations—it's also about honoring the principles of naturism itself. At its core, naturism promotes a profound connection with nature. Therefore, traveling sustainably is not only an ethical imperative but also a natural extension of our philosophy as naturists.

Start by considering the carbon footprint of your travel methods. International flights are often unavoidable, but there are ways to offset your carbon emissions. Many airlines now offer options to contribute to offset programs directly when you book your tickets. These programs invest in projects like reforestation, renewable energy, and conservation efforts that can mitigate the impact of your flight. For shorter journeys, consider using trains or buses, which typically emit fewer greenhouse gases compared to flying or driving.

Once you've arrived at your destination, make local choices to reduce your impact. Opt for eco-friendly accommodations—places that make use of renewable energy, water conservation, and waste reduction practices. Many naturist resorts and camps are increasingly committed to sustainability, making it easier for travelers to support eco-conscious businesses. Take the time to research your options, and consider staying in places that are certified by reputable environmental organizations.

While you're enjoying the natural surroundings, remember the Leave No Trace principles. These guidelines are especially important in naturist settings, where the goal is often to blend seamlessly with nature. Avoid disturbing local wildlife and plant life, and always clean up after yourself. In addition, consider carrying a reusable water bottle and other sustainable products to minimize waste.

When exploring your destinations, support local, eco-friendly businesses. Patronizing locally-owned restaurants and shops not only benefits the local economy but also often results in a smaller ecological footprint. These businesses are more likely to use local resources, reducing the need for long transportation chains that contribute to carbon emissions. Plus, you'll experience a more authentic taste of the local culture.

If you're participating in activities like hiking, swimming, or snorkeling, choose operators who prioritize environmental stewardship. Many tour companies now offer eco-tours, which not only reduce harm to the environment but also educate travelers about local ecosystems. Look for guides who are knowledgeable about conservation and are committed to minimizing the impact of their tours.

Another critical element to consider is waste management. Plastics, especially single-use plastics, are a significant problem worldwide. They can harm marine life, clog waterways, and take decades to break down. As a naturist traveler, bring reusable items whenever possible: bags, containers, and utensils. Avoid purchasing items packaged in plastic and consider returning or recycling waste items properly.

Water conservation is another vital practice. Many naturist spots, particularly those on islands or in arid regions, have limited freshwater resources. Be mindful of your water usage by taking shorter showers and reusing towels. Some resorts also have "grey water" systems that recycle water from sinks and showers for use in landscaping. Support these innovations by understanding and adhering to their guidelines.

Your diet can also reflect an environmentally conscious mindset. Eating less meat, for instance, can have a significant positive impact on the environment. The livestock industry is a major contributor to greenhouse gases, deforestation, and water use. Many destinations boast fresh, delicious fruits and vegetables, so take the opportunity to indulge in local, plant-based cuisine.

Moreover, consider volunteering your time as part of your vacation. Many naturist destinations offer opportunities to contribute to local conservation efforts, whether it's beach clean-ups, tree planting, or wildlife preservation projects. Engaging in these activities not only helps the environment but also provides a deeper connection to the place you're visiting.

Lastly, educating yourself and others is paramount. Share your experiences and the importance of sustainable travel with fellow naturists and travelers. The more people who are aware of and engaged in these practices, the greater the collective impact will be. Think of it as expanding the community's commitment to a philosophy that extends beyond just enjoying nature to actively protecting it.

By making conscientious choices, we not only preserve our beloved naturist destinations but also set an example for future travelers. Sustainable travel is an evolving journey, much like naturism itself. It involves continuous learning, adapting, and improving our practices. But the rewards—crystal-clear waters, lush landscapes, and thriving wildlife—are well worth the effort.

Supporting Local Communities

Traveling as a naturist goes beyond the enjoyment of picturesque dunes, serene beaches, and vibrant greenery. One of the foundational elements of sustainable and ethical naturist travel is the commitment to supporting local communities. When travelers consciously engage with and invest in the regions they explore, they foster a symbiotic relationship that benefits both the visitors and the locals. Understanding this dynamic can make a world of difference in your travel experience.

Choosing local businesses over international chains is one of the simplest yet most impactful ways to support the communities you're visiting. Whether it's staying in family-owned lodges, dining in small restaurants, or buying souvenirs directly from artisans, every dollar spent locally has a ripple effect. It helps maintain the economic stability of the area, and often, these small-scale businesses are more committed to environmentally friendly practices, aligning seamlessly with the ethos of naturist travel.

It's also enriching to delve into the cultural fabric of the destinations by participating in local events and traditions. Festivals, fairs, and community gatherings offer a plethora of experiences. You could find yourself dancing in a town square, learning traditional crafts, or savoring home-cooked meals that tell the stories of generations. These experiences foster a deeper connection to the place and its people, far beyond what typical tourist activities offer.

Connecting with local guides can further enhance your travel experience. They provide intimate knowledge of the area, including hidden naturist spots that may not be widely known. More importantly, they share the cultural and historical contexts that shape these landscapes. Touring with a local guide also means your money stays within the community, supporting livelihoods and preserving local traditions and stories for future generations.

In regions like South America's secluded escapes in Argentina or Brazil's coastal havens, engaging with the local populace can help sustain remote communities. Many of these areas rely heavily on tourism, and naturists traveling responsibly can make a significant positive impact. Imagine staying in an eco-lodge nestled in the Argentine wilderness, run by a family who shares tales of the land's natural and cultural history over an evening meal.

Volunteering is another profound way to give back. Naturist travel destinations often have opportunities for visitors to engage in community service, whether it's through organized programs or impromptu help. From beach clean-ups in Greece's idyllic isles to assisting in local community projects in Thailand's exotic freedom destinations, these acts of kindness can significantly improve local environments and foster goodwill.

However, supporting local communities isn't just about economic contributions. It's also about respecting and embracing their way of life. Naturist travelers should practice cultural sensitivities, ensuring their lifestyle choices do not disrupt local customs and traditions. For instance, in regions where naturism is still emerging or somewhat controversial, such as India's emerging spots or the hidden naturist paradises of Israel, it's critical to be mindful of local norms and sentiments.

Many naturist locations around the world are situated within or near environmentally sensitive areas. Thus, collaborating with local conservation groups can be incredibly rewarding. Participating in activities like tree planting, wildlife observation, and sustainable tourism practices helps preserve these precious ecosystems. Naturist tourists can become ambassadors of environmental stewardship, showcasing how a respectful, clothing-optional lifestyle can coexist harmoniously with nature.

The choice of accommodation can also reflect your commitment to supporting local communities. Opt for eco-friendly lodgings that employ local staff, utilize regional resources, and have systems in place to minimize their environmental footprint. Resorts and guesthouses that use solar power, rainwater harvesting, and local construction materials can provide a more authentic and conscious travel experience. In destinations like Costa del Sol in Spain or New Zealand's naturally free landscapes, eco-conscious accommodations often blend harmoniously with the naturist principle of being one with nature.

Engaging in meaningful exchanges with local artisans can provide a unique lens into a community's culture. Purchasing handmade crafts, art, or even food products directly supports the makers and reduces the environmental impact of mass production. These items often carry the spirit and essence of the place, serving as significant mementos of your naturist adventures. Imagine bringing home a piece of handcrafted jewelry from Morocco's emerging scene or artisanal pottery from a village in Corsica near its nude beaches.

For communities where naturism is a cornerstone of the local economy, such as France's Cap d'Agde or Croatia's islands, responsible travel practices ensure these destinations remain vibrant and welcoming. Participating in community-organized tours, workshops, and events fosters a sense of belonging and mutual respect. It transforms your journey from a mere vacation into a meaningful cultural exchange.

Moreover, consider supporting local conservation efforts. Many naturist travel spots are blessed with unique flora and fauna that require protection. Working with local NGOs, donating to environmental causes, or participating in conservation projects can leave a lasting legacy. Naturist travelers often cherish the natural beauty of the places they visit, and contributing to their preservation ensures that future generations can enjoy these pristine environments.

Language learning is another immersive way to engage and support local communities. Even basic phrases can go a long way in building rapport and showing respect. It demonstrates an interest in and appreciation for the local culture, breaking down barriers and fostering genuine connections. Imagine the joy of exchanging pleasantries in Spanish while exploring the naturist beaches of the Canary Islands or navigating a market in Turkey with a few well-learned Turkish phrases.

Respecting local regulations and participating in community dialogues about naturism can also be crucial. In areas where naturism is in developmental stages, understanding and adhering to guidelines ensures that the practice is perceived positively by the locals. This can pave the way for the broader acceptance and growth of naturism, creating more welcoming spaces for future travelers.

In more remote or rural areas, your visit can signal a broader economic benefit. Establishing positive relationships with locals in these less-trodden paths fosters both trust and understanding. It emphasizes that naturism and community development can go hand in hand. Your visit might inspire local initiatives, like small resorts or guided tour companies, enhancing the area's appeal for other travelers seeking genuine naturist experiences.

So, as you map out your next naturist adventure, remember that your choices have a ripple effect far beyond your immediate experience. Supporting local communities enriches your journey, fostering deep-rooted connections and ensuring the sustainability of the beautiful destinations you come to love. It's about mutual respect, shared joy, and a commitment to leaving each place just a little better than you found it. Let's embrace naturist travel not just as an exploration of the self but as a means to uplift and sustain the wondrous communities and environments that welcome us. You're not just a visitor but a steward of the places you explore.

Chapter 16:
Wellness and Naturism

Wellness and naturism intertwine seamlessly, offering a rejuvenating escape for the body and soul, far beyond the confines of conventional tourism. Picture yourself indulging in serene yoga sessions on a secluded beach, where the gentle whisper of the waves complements your breaths, grounding you to nature. Naturist destinations worldwide are increasingly embracing holistic wellness approaches, creating sanctuaries that promote mindfulness and relaxation in their purest forms. From meditative walks through verdant forests to invigorating spa treatments under open skies, the fusion of naturotherapy and wellness fosters a profound connection with both your inner self and the natural world. So, find yourself within the tranquil embrace of these idyllic retreats where every moment promises a harmonious blend of liberation and tranquility.

Mindfulness and Relaxation

Naturism and wellness share a profound connection, particularly when it comes to mindfulness and relaxation. Stripping away the barriers of clothing in serene environments naturally leads to a heightened sense of awareness and presence. Imagine the warm sun caressing your skin, the gentle breeze dancing around you, and the pure, unfiltered connection to nature. These vivid sensations offer a perfect backdrop for mindfulness practices.

Finding tranquility in naturist settings involves more than just physical freedom; it's about mental liberation as well. The practice of mindfulness, which involves being fully present in the moment, can be deepened by the naturist experience. Without the constraints of fabric and societal norms, you can embrace a sense of pure existence. Destinations around the globe offer these opportunities. Whether you're overlooking the azure waters of the Caribbean or the rugged coastlines of the Mediterranean, naturist spots become sanctuaries for mindfulness enthusiasts.

Consider starting your day with a sunrise meditation on a secluded nudist beach. The simple act of feeling the sand beneath your feet, the sound of waves breaking, and the sight of the horizon glowing can ground you in the present moment. These mindful experiences are not just rejuvenating but can also enhance your emotional well-being. Naturist retreats often incorporate these elements, providing designated quiet areas for meditation and reflection.

Exploring mindfulness in naturist environments doesn't stop at meditation. Engaging in deep breathing exercises, otherwise known as pranayama in yoga, becomes a more profound experience when you can feel every breath invigorating your being. As you breathe in deeply, you can sense the expansion of your ribcage without any restriction, and as you breathe out, the release feels more complete and cleansing. Pranayama coupled with the naturist lifestyle offers a unique pathway to inner peace.

Many naturist resorts also offer wellness programs that emphasize relaxation techniques. Think of guided relaxation sessions where trained instructors lead you through mental exercises designed to help you connect with your body and the surrounding environment. These sessions can help reduce stress, lower blood pressure, and boost your overall happiness. The natural settings in these resorts amplify the relaxation, making the experience not just beneficial but deeply transformative.

Another remarkable aspect of naturism is the ease with which you can engage in body-positive mindfulness practices. It's easier to accept and appreciate your body when you're surrounded by others who are also embracing their natural forms. This communal acceptance fosters a supportive environment where you can practice self-love and body gratitude. Here, the absence of judgment allows for a more profound and genuine connection to oneself.

Consider the simple act of walking through a naturist park. Known as nature walking in mindfulness circles, this activity becomes a vivid journey of discovery. Each step taken in the nude connects you to the elements—earth, wind, fire, and water—in an unmediated way. The sensation of grass underfoot or the tingle of a spritz of water from a nearby stream is amplified when you're not wearing shoes or clothes. It's about feeling alive and in harmony with the planet.

Then, there's the healing power of water. Naturist-friendly destinations with lakes, rivers, or ocean access often encourage mindful swimming. Allow yourself to float gently on the water's surface, feeling the liquid cradle and support your body. The mindful immersion in water, free from clothing, can quickly become a spiritual experience, as if you are becoming one with the element itself.

In addition to independent relaxation practices, naturism also lends itself beautifully to communal wellness activities. Many naturist resorts and retreats globally offer group sessions in practices like Tai Chi, a martial art known for its slow, deliberate movements promoting balance and inner peace. Participating in such activities nude not only enhances the physical benefits but also fosters a shared experience of tranquility among participants.

Practicing mindfulness and relaxation in naturist settings can fundamentally transform your travel experience. Naturist destinations invite you to slow down, tune in to your senses, and soak in the present moment. It's about embracing a holistic approach to well-being, one that integrates mind, body, and environment. Whether you're lounging by a naked pool in Mexico or embracing the rugged coastlines of Croatia, these places offer a sanctuary where you can unwind completely.

As you journey through various naturist destinations, take the time to explore different mindfulness techniques and discover what resonates with you. It's a personal journey, one where the aim is not just to relax but to rejuvenate and reconnect with your inner self. By integrating mindfulness and relaxation practices into your naturist travels, you create an experience that's not only liberating but also deeply fulfilling. So, uncover these hidden gems, both within the world and yourself, and let the essence of naturism guide you to a state of true relaxation and mindfulness.

Naturist Yoga and Meditation

Imagine starting your day with the gentle warmth of the morning sun on your bare skin as you extend into a deep stretch, feeling every muscle lengthen and awaken. Naturist yoga and meditation offer a unique path to wellness, merging the liberating practice of naturism with the profound benefits of mindful disciplines. This harmonious blend allows practitioners to reconnect with nature, their bodies, and their minds in a deeply rejuvenating way.

Yoga, in essence, promotes a deeper connection between the mind and the body, fostering a sense of inner peace and balance. When practiced in the nude, this connection can feel even more profound. By shedding clothes, you shed societal norms and constraints, which can be incredibly freeing. This act of baring it all isn't just physical; it's a spiritual and emotional experience that brings a heightened sense of liberation and acceptance.

Meditation, similarly, is a practice of stillness and introspection. In naturist meditation, this stillness is enhanced by the surrounding elements of nature—be it the sound of crashing waves, the rustle of leaves, or the calls of distant birds. Without the encumbrance of clothing, meditators often find a more profound connection to their environment, making the practice feel more integrated and holistic.

Whether you're a seasoned yogi or a newbie to naturism, starting with simple poses like the mountain pose or downward dog can help ease you into the practice. These foundational poses ground you and build strength and flexibility, preparing your body for more complex movements. As you progress, you might find yourself experimenting with poses that challenge your balance and core strength, like the tree pose or warrior series.

The surroundings can significantly enhance the naturist yoga experience. Many naturist resorts and retreats offer dedicated spaces for yoga practice—often outdoors with scenic views of the sea, mountains, or forests. Practicing yoga in such tranquil settings not only intensifies your connection to nature but also enhances the meditative aspects of each pose.

In these sanctuaries, morning yoga sessions synonymous with the rising sun can set a peaceful tone for the entire day. Evening sessions coincide with the setting sun, offering a perfect end to the day and helping to release any residual tension or stress. Each session becomes a celebration of the natural rhythms of the day and our place within them.

Beyond yoga, naturist meditation retreats provide an immersive experience designed to facilitate deeper levels of mindfulness and relaxation. Typically, these retreats include guided sessions that explore different meditation techniques such as mindfulness meditation, transcendental meditation, and guided imagery. By practicing mindfulness, participants are encouraged to remain present, fully engaging with each moment as it unfolds.

A naturist meditation session might begin with simple breathing exercises, focusing on inhaling and exhaling deeply to center the mind. As the session progresses, practitioners can delve into guided imagery or mindfulness exercises, where they are encouraged to observe their thoughts without judgment. The absence of clothing removes a layer of distraction, allowing for a more profound immersion into the meditative state.

One remarkable aspect of naturist yoga and meditation is the emphasis on community and shared experiences. Many retreats and resorts offer group classes, which foster a sense of camaraderie and mutual respect among participants. Engaging in these practices alongside others who share a commitment to naturism and wellness can amplify the benefits, creating a supportive environment for personal growth.

Throughout the world, numerous naturist resorts have recognized the growing demand for wellness activities and have responded by offering specialized yoga and meditation retreats. For instance, Europe boasts several renowned naturist yoga retreats, where practitioners can immerse themselves in daily yoga and meditation sessions set against breathtaking natural backdrops. In North America, locations such as California and Florida provide beautiful coastal settings that enhance the overall experience.

While traveling to these destinations, it's also essential to consider the cultural context and etiquette surrounding naturist practices. For instance, in some regions, nudity is embraced and deeply intertwined with local lifestyle and traditions, while in others, it may still be viewed with some degree of conservatism. Understanding and respecting these cultural nuances ensures that you can fully enjoy the benefits of naturist yoga and meditation without inadvertently offending local sensibilities.

Combining naturism with yoga and meditation also offers profound mental health benefits. The practice of mindfulness and self-acceptance inherent in both disciplines can significantly reduce feelings of stress and anxiety. Furthermore, the act of embracing your body—flaws and all—in a non-judgmental environment strengthens self-esteem and body positivity. Engaging in these practices can help dismantle entrenched insecurities, fostering a deep-seated sense of peace and self-worth.

For those planning a naturist vacation, integrating yoga and meditation into your itinerary can be a transformative experience. It offers an unparalleled opportunity to unwind, reset, and gain a profound appreciation for the world around you and within you. The sense of freedom and connection you'll experience can elevate your trip from a mere holiday to a journey of personal enlightenment.

In conclusion, naturist yoga and meditation represent a perfect fusion of physical, mental, and spiritual wellness. They invite you to explore beyond the superficial layers of life, into a space of genuine connection and holistic health. Whether you're practicing on a sun-drenched beach or a secluded forest glade, the blend of naturism with these ancient disciplines is a pathway to profound serenity and joy. Embrace the journey, breathe deeply, and let nature guide you toward an elevated state of being.

Chapter 17:
Family-friendly Naturist Vacations

Imagining a vacation where the whole family can enjoy the sun and sand without any clothing barriers brings a unique kind of freedom and connection. Family-friendly naturist vacations are designed to offer an environment where everyone, from toddlers to grandparents, can embrace the naturist lifestyle in safety and comfort. These destinations are not just about shedding clothes, but about creating spaces where body positivity and natural living flourish. Top venues offer sprawling beaches, child-friendly pools, and engaging activities that make it easy for families to bond and relax. From the serene shores of the Mediterranean to the welcoming resorts in North America, there are plenty of idyllic spots that cater specifically to families. Choosing the right destination ensures not only a fun-filled experience but also a meaningful one where your family can grow closer and experience a different pace of life, united under the sun.

Safe and Fun for Everyone

Planning a naturist vacation that includes every member of the family can seem like a tall order, but it's more attainable than one might expect. Family-friendly naturist resorts and destinations worldwide go to great lengths to ensure a welcoming, safe, and enjoyable environment for all ages. From meticulous childcare programs to engaging activities that captivate young minds, these vacation spots prove that naturism can indeed be a delightful family affair.

Many naturist resorts emphasize the importance of creating a secure atmosphere where families can feel comfortable and relaxed. Security measures such as check-in points and on-site staff ensure a safe environment. Parents can rest easy knowing that their children's safety is a top priority. Resorts often offer educational programs that teach kids about body positivity and respect for oneself and others, fostering a healthy perspective on naturism from a young age.

For families embarking on a naturist vacation, finding engaging activities that cater to diverse interests is crucial. Resorts and naturist destinations typically offer a wide variety of recreational options designed to entertain all age groups. From swimming pools and playgrounds to guided nature hikes and craft workshops, the opportunities for family bonding are plentiful. These activities not only keep everyone entertained but also help in developing a deeper connection with nature.

Swimming is often a highlight of naturist vacations, and many family-friendly resorts boast multiple pools catering to different age groups. Kiddie pools with shallow, safe water depths are perfect for toddlers, while larger pools with diving boards and water slides entertain older children and teens. Lifeguards are commonly present to ensure everyone's safety, allowing parents to enjoy their swim with peace of mind.

Beyond the swimming pool, sports and outdoor activities play a prominent role in most family-friendly naturist resorts. Tennis courts, volleyball nets, and mini-golf courses encourage active play and friendly competition. Nature trails and guided hikes offer educational experiences by exposing children to local flora and fauna, enriching their understanding of the natural world. Such experiences can be both relaxing and invigorating, making your vacation memorable.

Childcare services at many naturist resorts are exceptional. Trained professionals run kids' clubs and childcare centers, providing a range of age-appropriate activities. These clubs allow parents some much-needed downtime while ensuring that children are in a fun, supervised environment. Craft classes, storytelling sessions, and treasure hunts can keep the little ones engaged, giving parents a chance to relax and enjoy their own leisure activities.

Teenagers, often the hardest demographic to please while on vacation, will find their niche in family-friendly naturist settings as well. Teen clubs, social events, and adventure programs provide exciting activities tailored to the interests of young adults. Surfing lessons, zip-lining adventures, and beach volleyball tournaments offer thrills and opportunities to make new friends, ensuring that their vacation is anything but boring.

Mealtimes are another aspect where family-friendly naturist resorts shine. Dining facilities typically cater to the tastes and dietary requirements of children and adults alike. Buffets with kid-friendly options, special children's menus, and flexible mealtime schedules make it easy for families to enjoy meals together without the stress. Many resorts also organize themed dinners and barbecues, adding an extra layer of fun to the dining experience.

An important aspect of any family-oriented naturist vacation is the sense of community. Family-friendly naturist resorts often foster a communal atmosphere through social events, group activities, and community gatherings. This spirit of camaraderie makes it easier for families to interact with others, share experiences, and make lasting friendships. Regular events like talent shows, family game nights, and cultural festivals ensure there's never a dull moment, encouraging everyone to partake and enjoy.

Exploring the local culture and surroundings is another fantastic aspect of family-friendly naturist vacations. Excursions to nearby historical sites, museums, and natural landmarks can provide educational and enriching experiences for children and adults alike.

Resorts often organize guided tours, making it simple and safe for families to explore the area's unique offerings. Plus, these excursions allow for quality family time while learning something new and exciting together.

While planning a family naturist vacation, it's important to prepare your children and discuss what to expect. Open and honest conversations about the naturist lifestyle can help demystify the experience and make children feel more at ease. Emphasizing values such as respect, body positivity, and the enjoyment of nature can help set the tone for an enriching vacation.

It's also essential to maintain routines where possible. Bringing along favorite toys, books, and even bedding can help younger children feel more comfortable in a new setting. Setting aside time each day for familiar activities like reading bedtime stories or family games can provide a sense of normalcy amid the adventure.

Photographs are memories captured in frames, but at family-friendly naturist resorts, photography guidelines are usually strict to ensure privacy and comfort for all guests. With designated times and areas for capturing your precious family moments, it's reassuring to know that the privacy of your family is respected while still allowing you to document your cherished experiences.

In conclusion, naturist vacations offer an incredible opportunity for families to bond, explore, and embrace a healthier, more liberating way of life. With the right preparation and the perfect destination, a family-friendly naturist holiday can be one of the most joyful and fulfilling experiences you'll ever share. The wealth of activities catered to all ages, the sense of community, and the underlying message of body positivity make such vacations truly safe and fun for everyone.

Best Destinations for Families

When it comes to finding the perfect naturist retreat that caters to families, certain destinations worldwide stand out for their exceptional blend of comfort, safety, and the thrilling sense of adventure. These places have cultivated a peaceful environment where naturism is not simply accepted but embraced with open arms, fostering a nurturing atmosphere perfect for every member of the family, regardless of their age. From idyllic beaches to luxurious resorts, these destinations are not only naturist-friendly but also family-centric, offering a seamless blend of relaxation and fun.

One standout spot is the French Riviera, specifically Cap d'Agde. Widely recognized as the world's largest naturist village, Cap d'Agde isn't just a haven for naturist enthusiasts but also a wonderful family-friendly destination. Stretching along the Azure Mediterranean coast, it offers a variety of accommodation options, from family-friendly resorts to holiday villages designed with children in mind. Play areas, swimming pools, and organized activities ensure kids are entertained, while parents can relax and enjoy the natural beauty of the surroundings.

Across the Atlantic, in the United States, a gem awaits on the shores of Florida. Haulover Beach in Miami is one of the most famous nude beaches in the country and it is exceptionally family-friendly. Security and lifeguards on duty provide an added layer of safety, while picnic spots and nearby amenities cater to family needs. The beach organizes regular events and activities that encourage families to engage and interact in a safe, nudist-friendly environment.

Heading deeper into the heart of Europe, Croatia's Dalmatian Coast offers stunning naturist retreats that welcome families with true Mediterranean warmth. The island of Rab, known as one of the pioneers of naturism in Croatia, provides serene, family-friendly beaches where the water is shallow and clear, making it perfect for younger children to play safely. Additionally, many resorts in this area offer kids' activities and family-centric amenities, ensuring both parents and children have a memorable stay.

Germany is another family-friendly naturist destination and boasts some of the best facilities designed specifically for family naturist vacations. The Baltic Sea, in particular, is home to several naturist resorts and beaches. Darßer Weststrand, one of Germany's most well-known nudist beaches, provides a safe and welcoming environment where families can enjoy a variety of outdoor activities like beach volleyball, sandcastle building, and cycling. Resorts in the region often come equipped with playgrounds, kids' clubs, and swimming pools, making it a haven for family vacations.

Venturing southward, Greece offers a host of naturist havens, with Crete being especially notable for its family-friendly spirit. The island's laid-back vibe and welcoming locals make it a natural fit for families. Filaki Beach, near the town of Chora Sfakion, is specifically designated for naturists and offers a serene setting away from the more crowded tourist spots. Cretan naturist resorts nearby offer family-friendly accommodations, with activities designed for younger guests, ensuring that children are entertained and safe while parents can relax in the sun.

Portugal's Algarve region is yet another splendid destination for naturist families. Skinny-dipping in Portugal's warm waters is played out best in places like Praia do Barril in Tavira. Known for its pristine sands and tranquil ambiance, the beach is ideal for a family day out. The region also boasts numerous naturist-friendly resorts with excellent facilities for children including pools, kids' clubs, and organized family activities.

Costa Natura in Southern Spain stands as a premier family-friendly naturist resort. Located in Estepona, it offers a range of family-oriented amenities, including swimming pools, play areas, and even a children's animation team that organizes various activities to keep the younger ones entertained. The resort prides itself on a community atmosphere, making it easy for families to mix and mingle.

For those looking to combine a cultural experience with their naturist vacation, Japan's Shizuoka Prefecture offers a unique and enriching family-friendly naturist experience. While naturism as a lifestyle isn't widespread in Japan, certain retreats cater specifically to family-style naturism with a focus on wellbeing and relaxation. These retreats are well-equipped with hot springs, traditional Japanese gardens, and family activities that immerse visitors in the tranquil beauty of Japanese nature while adhering to naturist principles.

Venturing to New Zealand, the country's North Island, specifically Waiheke Island, presents itself as a fantastic destination for naturist families. Renowned for its lush landscapes and secluded beaches, Waiheke provides a serene and family-friendly backdrop. Little Palm Beach is a naturist spot where families can enjoy the clear waters and beautiful scenery in peace. Nearby accommodations offer family rooms and kid-friendly amenities, making it a stress-free getaway for families.

Finally, Australia offers a wealth of naturist destinations perfect for families. From the coastal gems near Sydney to the vast beauties of Queensland's Sunshine Coast, there's something for every family. Lady Bay Beach in Sydney and Alexandria Bay in Noosa are renowned for their naturist-friendly atmospheres and family-friendly facilities. Resorts in these areas cater to families with amenities such as large pools, organized kids' activities, and childcare services.

In essence, the world is filled with extraordinary naturist destinations that prioritize family-friendly environments. These places understand the balance required to offer a safe, fun, and liberating vacation for families who are eager to embrace naturism. Each destination not only provides the basics but also enriches the experience with additional elements that cater specifically to the needs of diverse family units, making sure that both parents and children have an unforgettable and rejuvenating time. By choosing any of these splendid locations, families can create lasting memories, strengthening their bond through the liberating spirit of naturism.

Chapter 18:
Solo Naturist Travel

Embarking on a solo naturist journey can be one of the most liberating adventures you'll ever experience. As you shed your clothes, you also shed societal expectations and embark on a voyage of self-discovery. Traveling alone offers the freedom to create your own itinerary, explore at your own pace, and immerse yourself in the serene beauty of naturist destinations without distractions. Imagine waking up to the sound of waves on a secluded beach or hiking through a sun-drenched forest, your only company being the profound sense of connection with nature. This chapter is designed to equip you with essential safety tips and confidence-building strategies, so you can fully embrace the thrills and challenges of solo naturist travel. By the end, you'll be ready to uncover hidden gems across the globe while savoring the unique sense of empowerment that comes from journeying alone.

Safety Tips and Confidence

Embarking on a solo naturist journey can be one of the most liberating and self-affirming experiences you'll ever encounter. But like any adventure, it comes with its own set of challenges and considerations, especially when you're traveling alone. The key to a successful trip lies in being prepared while maintaining a confident and positive mindset. This section will delve into essential safety tips tailored for the solo naturist traveler, and how to nurture the confidence needed to make your journey unforgettable.

First and foremost, always inform someone you trust about your travel itinerary. Share details like the destinations you're visiting, your accommodation information, and key contact numbers. This act of precaution ensures that someone is aware of your whereabouts, providing an added layer of safety. With today's technology, it's easier than ever to stay connected; a quick message or email update can make all the difference.

Avoiding isolated or unknown areas at night is another crucial safety tip. Although the allure of a moonlit beach can be incredibly tempting, it's wise to stick to well-lit and commonly frequented areas when the sun goes down. Opt for places known for their safety and popularity among naturists. Researching beforehand can give you insights into which spots are naturist-friendly and safe. Online forums and reviews are invaluable for this purpose.

Understanding the local customs and legalities is vital. While naturism is embraced in many parts of the world, some regions may have specific regulations or cultural sensitivities regarding public nudity. Ignorance of these laws can lead to misunderstandings or, worse, legal trouble. Familiarize yourself with local rules and norms to ensure your naturist practices are welcomed and respected.

Building confidence in your naturist journey starts with embracing yourself just as you are. For many, the initial step of disrobing in a public setting is daunting. It's completely natural to feel apprehensive. Remember, confidence grows with practice and experience. Start in environments where you feel the most comfortable—perhaps at a well-reviewed naturist resort or beach known for its inclusive and supportive culture.

It's also essential to cultivate a positive mindset. Focus on the liberating aspects of naturism: the sense of being one with nature, the freedom of shedding societal constraints, and the profound connection you feel with your surroundings. These experiences often overshadow initial nerves, paving the way for bolder and more fulfilling adventures.

Another effective way to build confidence is by connecting with other naturists. Joining online communities or social media groups dedicated to naturist travel can offer support, advice, and encouragement. Engaging in discussions, asking questions, and sharing experiences can help alleviate any fears or doubts you might have. It's reassuring to know you're part of a broader, welcoming community.

Self-care is paramount when traveling solo. Always carry essentials like water, snacks, and a basic first aid kit. These items can be lifesavers, especially in remote locations. Additionally, keep your phone charged and consider investing in a portable charger. In unexpected situations, staying connected can provide a lifeline.

Confidence also stems from self-reliance and preparedness. Trust your instincts—if a situation feels off, it's perfectly okay to leave. Your comfort and safety should always be your top priority. This principle applies to interactions with others, too. If someone makes you feel uneasy, don't hesitate to distance yourself or seek assistance from authorities or fellow naturists.

Attending workshops or events focused on naturist practices can also boost your confidence. These gatherings usually cover a range of topics, from naturist etiquette and self-acceptance to practical tips on staying safe. They provide a supportive environment where you can learn and grow, surrounded by like-minded individuals.

Lastly, take the time to celebrate your journey and accomplishments. Solo travel, especially in the naturist realm, is a bold step that not only broadens your horizons but also deepens your sense of self. Whether you're enjoying a secluded beach or a bustling naturist resort, each experience contributes to your personal growth and confidence. Rejoice in your courage and the unique adventure you're crafting.

In conclusion, solo naturist travel is a remarkably enriching experience that balances the thrill of exploration with the quiet joy of self-discovery. By prioritizing safety, preparing thoroughly, and nurturing a confident mindset, you're on the path to not just seeing new places, but also embracing and celebrating your authentic self. This journey is yours to shape, filled with endless possibilities and the pure, unfiltered beauty of naturism.

Making the Most of Your Solo Adventure

Setting off on a solo naturist adventure can feel like a bold move, but it offers an unparalleled opportunity to connect with yourself and nature. The experience is intensely personal, allowing you to shed not just your clothes but also societal expectations and stresses. There's a unique sense of freedom in wandering pristine beaches or hidden trails, experiencing the world in your most natural state.

The first step to making the most of your solo journey is preparation. Knowing the lay of the land helps you feel more comfortable and confident. Do a bit of research about your chosen destination—understanding local customs and naturist etiquette can make a big difference. Dive into naturist communities online where seasoned travelers share tips and experiences. You'll find a wealth of information that'll make your solo adventure smoother and more enjoyable.

Confidence is key to enjoying your time alone. It's natural to feel a bit self-conscious at first, but remember, everyone at these naturist spots is there for the same reason—an appreciation for freedom and nature. Build your confidence by starting with smaller, quieter destinations before venturing to bustling naturist resorts. Over time, your comfort zone will expand, and you'll be ready to explore more vibrant locales.

Your solo adventure is a time to focus on self-care and mindfulness. Traveling alone means you have the luxury to set your own pace and agenda. Wake up early to witness the sunrise, take leisurely swims, or spend your afternoons reading a book under the shade of a tree. Use this time to indulge in activities that nourish your soul. Incorporate moments of meditation and yoga to enhance your relaxation.

Engage with the local culture as much as possible. Learning a few phrases in the native language can go a long way in enhancing your interactions. Locals often appreciate the effort and will be more open to sharing hidden gems of their region with you. Take time to explore nearby towns, savor local cuisine, and visit markets. This not only enriches your travel experience but also provides an avenue to understand the cultural context surrounding naturism in the area.

Record your journey. Whether it's through a travel journal, photography, or a personal blog, documenting your experiences can be incredibly fulfilling. These records will not only serve as cherished memories but can also offer insights when you reflect on your journey. Plus, sharing your story might inspire others to embrace the beauty and liberation of solo naturist travel.

Safety is paramount when traveling alone, especially in less familiar territories. Always inform someone you trust about your daily plans and check in regularly. Equip yourself with a reliable map, keep emergency contacts handy, and be aware of your surroundings. Trust your instincts—if something doesn't feel right, it probably isn't. It's better to err on the side of caution.

Socializing when solo doesn't have to be daunting. Many naturist resorts and camps organize group activities such as guided tours, fitness classes, or art workshops. These activities are fantastic opportunities to meet like-minded individuals while still enjoying your solo experience. Who knows? You might make lifelong friends along the way.

Look beyond the designated naturist spots. Some of the most picturesque and peaceful places might be off the beaten path. Explore secluded areas like forest trails, hidden lakes, or deserted beaches. Always ensure these locations are safe and permissible for naturist activities, and respect the environment by leaving no trace.

Don't underestimate the power of spontaneity. While planning is crucial, leaving room for spontaneous adventures can add an unexpected thrill to your journey. Perhaps you stumble upon a local festival or find an inviting cove that wasn't on your itinerary. Embrace these unplanned moments—they often create the most memorable experiences.

Lastly, remember to enjoy the solitude. There is immense joy in being alone in nature, unencumbered by the presence of others. It's a chance to reconnect with your inner self, to listen to your thoughts, and to find peace in your own company. Use this time to reflect, to dream, and to simply be. Your solo naturist adventure is not just a trip; it's a journey towards self-discovery and inner freedom.

Chapter 19:
Group Naturist Trips

Embarking on a group naturist trip offers an unparalleled sense of camaraderie and shared liberation that turns each journey into an unforgettable adventure. Imagine soaking in sun-drenched vistas and pristine beaches alongside like-minded individuals who share your passion for naturism. Organizing these trips might seem daunting, but the sense of community and deep connections formed make it worthwhile. From the lively shores of Cap d'Agde to the serene retreats in Greece, the world is your oyster when it comes to choosing the perfect destination. Many of these locales are tailored for socializing, offering communal activities and events that encourage bonding and collective joy. Whether you're navigating through enchanting coastal paths or sharing meals under the open sky, group naturist trips pave the way for an enriched and delightful travel experience.

Organizing Group Travels

Traveling as a group can be a richly rewarding experience, especially when it comes to naturist trips. Whether you're planning a getaway with close friends or organizing a retreat for a larger community, the benefits of shared adventures are manifold. Being surrounded by like-minded individuals who share your passion for naturism only enhances the sense of liberation and connection you feel.

Organizing a group naturist trip, however, requires thoughtful planning and coordination. You need to ensure that everyone's expectations are met and that the chosen destination caters to the collective desires. Start by gauging interest within your community or circle of friends. Send out feelers to see who would be keen on a group trip and what kind of activities and locations excite them the most. Some may be ardent sun-worshippers who prefer beach settings, while others might seek the solace of a naturist retreat nestled in nature.

Once you've gauged interest, it's crucial to establish a budget. Group travels often offer the advantage of shared costs, which can make exotic destinations more accessible. From accommodations to transportation, bulk booking can result in substantial savings. Yet, it's important to be transparent about the financial expectations from the beginning to avoid any misunderstandings later on.

After aligning on a budget, selecting the right destination is the next pivotal step. This will largely depend on the group's preferences, but it's wise to consider locations that offer a mix of activities, such as hiking, swimming, and cultural excursions. This ensures that everyone in the group has ample opportunities to immerse themselves in the experiences they cherish. Additionally, choosing naturist-friendly destinations that have well-established communities can provide a welcoming and comfortable environment for first-timers and seasoned naturists alike.

When planning the itinerary, flexibility becomes your best ally. While it's helpful to have a structured schedule, allowing room for spontaneous activities and rest is essential. This balance ensures that the trip doesn't become an overwhelming marathon but remains a rejuvenating escape for all members involved. For many, part of the allure of naturism is the unhurried pace and the freedom to connect with nature and themselves, so the itinerary should reflect this ethos.

Communication is paramount in the lead-up to the trip. Regular updates via email or a group chat can keep everyone informed about bookings, itinerary changes, and other essential details. Defaulting to a single person as the trip coordinator can streamline communications and decision-making processes. This role could entail everything from handling bookings and payments to mediating any arising issues, so it's important that the coordinator is both organized and approachable.

While on the trip, maintaining respect and understanding within the group is essential. Everyone has different levels of comfort with naturism, and it's important to create an environment where everyone feels safe and respected. Establishing guidelines, such as respecting personal space and remaining conscious of group dynamics, can ensure a harmonious experience for all participants.

It's also worth considering the logistics of meals and accommodations. Group stays can vary from shared villas and house rentals to individual rooms within a dedicated naturist resort. Establishing a meal plan—whether that's cooking together in a communal kitchen or dining at local naturist-friendly restaurants—can add to the sense of community and shared experience.

Planning group activities that emphasize the naturist lifestyle can further enrich the trip. From group yoga sessions at sunrise to engaging in mindfulness exercises against the backdrop of serene landscapes, these activities can foster a deeper connection with naturism for everyone involved. Organize excursions that explore the local culture and natural beauty of your destination, always in a manner that respects the local customs and environment.

As you plan out your trip, consider the environmental impact of your travels. Opt for eco-friendly accommodations and minimize waste by reducing plastic use and recycling. These small but significant actions can make a big difference, helping to preserve the natural beauty of the destinations you visit.

Safety is another critical factor. Ensuring the health and well-being of all group members should be at the forefront of your planning.

Have a first aid kit at hand and be aware of the nearest medical facilities. Make sure everyone has adequate travel insurance that covers naturist activities and international travel. It's better to be prepared and not need it, than to need it and not be prepared.

Finally, keep the spirit of adventure alive. Group naturist trips offer a unique opportunity to bond with others over shared passions and create lasting memories. By thoughtfully organizing and respecting the needs and desires of everyone in the group, you'll be able to craft an unforgettable experience that celebrates the essence of naturism and camaraderie.

Planning such a trip can indeed be a bit of a logistical challenge, but the rewards are incomparable. There's nothing quite like the collective joy of discovering a hidden beach, sharing stories under the stars, or simply basking in the warmth of the sun without any barriers. It's these moments of connection, both with each other and nature, that make group naturist travels a truly special adventure.

Best Destinations for Socializing

When embarking on group naturist trips, finding the perfect destination where everyone can feel comfortable, connect, and socialize can make all the difference. Lucky for us, the world is brimming with places that offer not just stunning landscapes and serenity but vibrant communities that welcome naturists with open arms. These destinations invite you to not only shed your clothes but also to let go of your inhibitions and bond with fellow travelers in a uniquely liberating way.

Cap d'Agde in France stands out as a quintessential spot for naturist socializing. This village is often dubbed the "Naked City" for good reason—its entire infrastructure is designed to support a carefree, clothes-free atmosphere. Imagine wandering through bustling markets, sunbathing on expansive beaches, or enjoying a meal at a seaside café, all in the nude. The inclusive and jovial atmosphere makes it easy for groups to mingle and meet like-minded individuals. It offers a perfect blend of relaxation and activity, with options ranging from water sports to naturist-themed nightclubs.

Spain's Costa del Sol offers another exceptional location for naturist groups. Known for its sun-kissed beaches and friendly locals, this region blends the best of relaxation and socializing. Playa El Mago, one of the area's famous nude beaches, provides a serene environment where groups can bask in the Mediterranean sun or participate in social events hosted by local naturist groups. The beachside bars and eateries serve as excellent spots to engage in conversations and make new friends, making it a must-visit for naturist travelers seeking a sociable yet laid-back experience.

Heading over to the Caribbean, Jamaica's nude beaches are legendary among naturist circles. Resorts like Hedonism II in Negril aren't just about beaches; they are social hotspots filled with themed nights, pool parties, and organized excursions. Here, every day brings opportunities to mingle, dance, and share stories with naturists from around the globe. The vibe is casual and relaxed, making it an excellent choice for groups looking to bond over sun, sea, and shared experiences.

In North America, the West Coast of the USA offers a string of naturist-friendly spots that balance natural beauty and social activities. Haulover Beach in Miami is a standout, known for its relaxed regulations and welcoming environment. It's an ideal setting for group outings where you can join in on beach volleyball, yoga sessions, or simply relax and chat under the Florida sun. The beach community is friendly and open, providing ample opportunities for social interaction.

If your group is more inclined towards a laid-back, natural setting, then British Columbia in Canada may be just the place. Wreck Beach in Vancouver is not only a breathtaking spot with its stunning views and pristine waters but also a social haven. It's frequented by a diverse array of naturists who come together to relax, play music, and join in communal gatherings. There's a real sense of camaraderie here, making it an excellent destination for groups looking to immerse themselves in nature and each other's company.

South of the border, Mexico offers some stellar options for naturist socializing as well. Zipolite Beach in Oaxaca is one of the few officially recognized nude beaches in the country. This bohemian paradise is known for its welcoming atmosphere and vibrant social scene. The annual Zipolite Nudist Festival draws naturists from all over, featuring activities, workshops, and parties that make it a great spot for groups to connect and celebrate naturism.

Venturing to the Southern Hemisphere, Australia's Queensland Coasts provide ample opportunities for group naturist activities. Alexandria Bay in Noosa National Park is a standout, known for its beautiful landscapes and vibrant community events. The naturist events held here often include beach games, picnics, and even group hikes, ensuring that there's always something to bring people together and foster connections.

One can't overlook the Mediterranean's offerings either. Greece's Naturist resorts, such as those found on the idyllic isles of Crete, are famous for their hospitality and social potential. The tranquil environment of the Greek isles, combined with the excellent facilities, makes them ideal for group activities ranging from group dinners under the stars to daytime excursions exploring the historical ruins and stunning seascapes. There's a sense of timeless beauty here, making social interactions feel even more enchanting.

Croatia's coastline also deserves mention, particularly the naturist campsites dotting the Adriatic Sea. Locations like Koversada in Istria offer beautifully maintained resorts where naturists can enjoy a variety of activities such as group sailing, beach yoga, or simply sharing meals in communal dining areas. These settings provide numerous chances for naturist groups to create lasting memories while enjoying one another's company.

Italy presents endless thrilling options, especially in its enchanting Sardinia region. Known for its pristine beaches and inviting waters, Sardinia is a gem for naturist travelers. Group activities can range from snorkeling in the clear waters to group tours exploring the island's rich history. The natural beauty combined with the friendly local culture ensures that groups have plenty of opportunities to socialize in meaningful ways.

In the heart of Eastern Europe, Bulgaria offers a uniquely untamed naturist experience. Areas along the Black Sea, such as Vaya Beach, are becoming increasingly popular for group naturist trips. These destinations offer a raw, uncommercialized beauty and a budding naturist community you can easily plug into. This burgeoning scene means that groups can not only enjoy the unspoiled landscapes but also actively participate in shaping and growing the naturist culture.

Israel's secret beaches, like those around the Dead Sea, offer tranquil settings where naturist groups can bond in serene, secluded environments. The Dead Sea's unique saline waters provide a therapeutic experience while communal areas encourage social interaction. Naturist groups can come together for shared wellness routines, sunset gatherings, or simply floating together in the buoyant waters, fostering a sense of connection and community.

India is slowly but surely emerging on the global naturist map, with Goa's beaches providing a welcoming environment for group naturist trips. Here, groups can relax on expansive sandy shores, participate in beach yoga sessions, or explore the rich cultural landscape together. The communal vibes of beachside shacks and open-air gatherings make it easy for group members to socialize and form lasting relationships.

There's something truly magical about finding a place where you can feel completely at ease, not just in your own skin but also in the company of others. These destinations, with their unique blend of natural beauty and social opportunities, offer naturist groups the perfect backdrop for creating unforgettable experiences and building bonds that will last a lifetime. So gather your friends, pack your essentials, and set off to discover these meccas of naturist socializing.

Chapter 20:
Naturist Cruises: Freedom at Sea

Setting sail on a naturist cruise offers a unique blend of liberation and adventure, inviting travelers to experience the world from the comfort of a floating paradise. Imagine sunbathing on the open deck under a clear azure sky, the refreshing sea breeze caressing your skin, free from the constraints of clothing. These specialized cruises cater to both seasoned naturists and newcomers, providing an atmosphere of acceptance and unity. As the ship glides through crystalline waters, stops at secluded, breathtaking locations further enhance the feeling of complete freedom. Onboard, you'll find a vibrant community, with like-minded individuals embracing the naturist lifestyle, contributing to an unforgettable and rejuvenating adventure at sea.

Major Cruise Lines and Routes

The sense of freedom and adventure that comes with naturist cruises is unparalleled. Major cruise lines have taken note and now offer specialized voyages that cater to the naturist community. Sailing across open waters with the wind in your hair and the sun kissing your skin provides an exhilarating sense of liberation. Among the major players in naturist cruises, you will find a few that have carved their niches serving this unique segment of travelers, ensuring that their experiences are not only memorable but deeply enriching.

Bare Necessities is one of the pioneers in the naturist cruise industry. Established in the 1990s, this company has grown exponentially, offering a wide array of itineraries across different parts of the globe. You can embark on cruises that traverse the Caribbean, with stops at idyllic islands where naturist beaches are aplenty. Imagine anchoring off the coast of Jamaica, where the famous Seven Mile Beach allows for au naturel lounging, or exploring the hidden coves of the Bahamas. Bare Necessities is well-known for creating a comfortable and welcoming environment for naturists of all stripes, whether seasoned veterans or first-timers.

Bliss Cruise is another name you're likely to come across when researching naturist voyages. Though slightly more niche, focusing on adult-only sailings, Bliss Cruise combines the luxurious amenities of modern cruise ships with a laid-back naturist atmosphere. Their sailings often include stops in the Mediterranean, where you can stroll nude along the enchanting beaches of France's Cap d'Agde or Italy's serene Sardinia. Bliss Cruise ensures that each stop is curated carefully to enhance the naturist experience, providing not just beautiful landscapes but also enriching cultural encounters.

In a different vein, there's the Caliente Resorts Cruise. Known for their land-based naturist resorts, Caliente has expanded into the waters, offering voyages that reflect their commitment to luxury and relaxation. These cruises often highlight destinations closer to home, such as the pristine waters of the Florida Keys, providing a perfect getaway for North American naturists who prefer shorter, yet fulfilling voyages. With an emphasis on wellness, you can partake in onboard yoga sessions, meditation, and other activities designed to rejuvenate both the body and spirit.

SeaDream Yacht Club, while not exclusively a naturist line, offers private charters that allow for a completely customized naturist experience. Renting a luxurious mega-yacht can offer an intimate and tailor-made journey across the Adriatic, visiting Croatia's stunning naturist beaches, or along the Greek Isles' most secluded shores. This option provides unparalleled privacy and exclusivity, ideal for naturist friends or families looking for an intimate and luxurious naturist escape.

The routes taken by these naturist cruises are as varied as the participants themselves. The Caribbean remains a perennial favorite, with its temperate climate, clear blue waters, and numerous naturist-friendly beaches. Routes through Eastern and Western Europe provide a different flavor of naturist travel, combining rich history and culture with stunning natural landscapes. Mediterranean cruises offer a blend of picturesque coastal towns and ancient ruins, all easily accessible from the ship. Imagine basking in the Mediterranean sun as you sail toward the storied shores of Greece or the unspoiled beauty of Croatia's islands.

For a more exotic flair, some cruises chart a course through South East Asia, with stops in Thailand's Phuket and Koh Samui. Here, the lush tropical landscapes and secluded bays provide a perfect backdrop for naturist freedom. Each destination brings its own set of attractions and experiences, from exploring ancient temples to diving into vibrant coral reefs, all while enjoying the freedom of naturism.

The social aspect of naturist cruises can't be understated. Friendships are easily formed during these laid-back voyages, where like-minded individuals share in the adventure and liberation that comes with being at sea without the confines of clothing. Events and activities are planned not only to entertain but also to foster connections among travelers. From themed parties to group excursions, there's always an opportunity to bond over shared interests and experiences.

When considering your next naturist cruise, it's worth noting the variety of ships available. Large ocean liners, replete with every conceivable amenity, offer endless entertainment options and multiple dining experiences. Mid-sized ships strike a balance, often providing a more intimate atmosphere while still offering a wealth of activities. For those seeking a more personal experience, private yacht charters or smaller boutique cruises focus on luxury and exclusivity, allowing for a higher degree of freedom and customization.

Booking your trip through these major cruise lines ensures not only a well-maintained vessel and professional crew but a community-oriented environment where naturism is celebrated and respected. The key to a successful naturist cruise is the atmosphere of acceptance and camaraderie that allows every guest to feel at ease, from the moment they board until they disembark.

In the end, naturist cruises offer a unique and liberating way to explore the world. The routes chosen by these major cruise lines take you through some of the most beautiful and naturist-friendly destinations on the planet, ensuring your journey is both breathtaking and freeing. As you sail across turquoise waters and visit sandy shores, the experience of a naturist cruise will resonate as a highlight in your adventures, a testament to the true freedom found at sea.

Tips for First-time Cruisers

Setting sail on a naturist cruise is a liberating and exhilarating experience, but it can also be daunting if it's your first time. The thought of being surrounded by fellow naturists in the close quarters of a ship might stir a mixture of excitement and nerves. Here are some useful tips to make your maiden voyage as smooth and enjoyable as possible.

First and foremost, choose the right cruise line. There are several major companies that specialize in naturist cruises, each offering a unique experience. Consider what you're looking for—whether it's a relaxed, intimate vibe or a bustling social scene—and research the different options. Look into the itinerary, the onboard activities, and the type of passengers the cruise attracts. Making an informed choice can set the stage for a fantastic journey.

Once you've booked your cruise, start planning your packing list. While it's tempting to think packing is minimal because you'll be in the buff most of the time, there are still essentials you shouldn't overlook. Besides the usual travel documents, remember to pack plenty of sunscreen. Opt for coral reef-safe products to minimize environmental impact. You'll also want to bring comfortable footwear for onboard activities and shore excursions. Don't forget a few outfits for any non-naturist events or formal nights that might be part of the cruise.

Understanding and respecting naturist etiquette is crucial. Being well-versed in the do's and don'ts will help you feel more at ease and prevent any awkward situations. For instance, always carry a towel to sit on—it's a widespread and appreciated custom among naturists. When interacting with others, maintaining eye contact can go a long way in fostering respectful and comfortable conversations. Avoid taking photos without explicit permission to respect everyone's privacy.

As you embark on this extraordinary journey, it's important to stay open-minded and flexible. Naturist cruises attract a diverse group of people, each with different backgrounds and reasons for embracing the naturist lifestyle. Embrace the opportunity to meet new people, share experiences, and learn from one another. Whether you're an extrovert or an introvert, there's a space for you to feel included and respected.

Participate in onboard activities to enhance your cruise experience. Most naturist cruises offer an array of activities ranging from yoga classes at sunrise to dance parties under the stars. Joining in these activities can help you socialize and make lasting memories. If you're traveling solo, this is an excellent way to break the ice and find your tribe among fellow travelers.

Don't forget to take advantage of the shore excursions. These cruises often dock at some of the most breathtaking and naturist-friendly destinations in the world. From secluded beaches to adventurous hiking trails, these excursions offer the perfect blend of exploration and relaxation. Make sure to check the packing requirements for these day trips, as some may require specific footwear or gear.

Mental preparation is just as important as your physical preparation. It's normal to have reservations about nudity, but remember that everyone on the cruise is in the same boat—literally and figuratively. Embrace the freedom and release any insecurities. The naturist community is known for its acceptance and body positivity, making it the perfect environment for shedding those societal norms and embracing your authentic self.

Stay hydrated! Being at sea and in the sun can be dehydrating. Drink plenty of water throughout the day to stay energized and healthy. Most cruises offer abundant fresh water options, but bringing a refillable water bottle is always a good idea.

Communicate with the crew if you have any questions or concerns. The staff on naturist cruises are usually well-trained and very approachable. They understand the unique dynamics of naturist travel and are there to ensure you have a pleasant and worry-free experience. Don't hesitate to ask them about onboard facilities, activities, or safety procedures.

It's also good to familiarize yourself with the ship's layout early on. Knowing where the pools, dining areas, and activity zones are can save you time and make your cruise more enjoyable. Many ships offer guided tours on the first day to help passengers get acquainted with their new surroundings—take advantage of this.

Lastly, savor the moments. A naturist cruise is not just a vacation; it's a journey of self-discovery and liberation. Feel the wind on your skin, the sun's warmth, and the soothing sounds of the ocean. Reflect on the simplicity and beauty of nature, and let the freedom at sea fill you with a sense of peace and joy. Whether you're lounging on the deck or exploring a hidden cove, each moment offers a chance to connect more deeply with yourself and the world around you.

Remember, the aim of naturist travel is not only the absence of clothing but the presence of freedom, authenticity, and respect. As you step aboard your first naturist cruise, let go of societal expectations and embrace the unique adventure ahead. With an open heart and a spirited curiosity, you are poised to have an unforgettable experience at sea.

Chapter 21:
Naturist Festivals and Events

Naturist festivals and events are vibrant celebrations that bring together enthusiasts from all walks of life, transforming serene landscapes into buzzing hubs of shared freedom and joy. Scattered across the globe, these gatherings offer an unparalleled opportunity to connect with a community that values body positivity and the uninhibited pleasure of being one with nature. Picture the carefree atmosphere of the World Naked Bike Ride, where participants pedal through city streets with infectious glee, or the electrifying castaway experience at the Nudefest in the UK, where workshops, live music, and beachfront camaraderie set the stage for unforgettable memories. From Croatia's lush Adriatic islands to Australia's sunny expanses, each festival not only allows you to immerse yourself in the liberating ethos of naturism but also introduces you to the local culture and scenic beauty of your chosen destination. Whether it's under the midnight sun of Scandinavia or the tropical charm of Brazil, naturist events are a reminder that the best adventures are those where you leave everything behind and embrace the world as nature intended.

Celebrations Around the Globe

Numerous cultures celebrate the human body in its most natural form through festivals that highlight the collective exhilaration of nudity. Around the world, naturist celebrations integrate traditions, local customs, and everything from fun activities to spiritual rituals. Each event provides a unique lens through which to view naturist lifestyles, embodying a colorful tapestry of human expression and acceptance.

In Southern Europe, the annual *Naked Bike Ride* spans numerous countries. It isn't just a festival but also a statement for body positivity and environmental consciousness. Cyclists gather, often in the thousands, to ride through urban centers, shedding their clothes along with their inhibitions. Paint and glittered bodies wind through historic streets, transforming urban landscapes into living canvases. These rides are not just local phenomena; they take place in cities as varied as Thessaloniki and Madrid, making them substantial spectacles for both participants and onlookers.

Switching gears to the beaches of France, the naturist capital of the world hosts some of the most iconic events. The town of Cap d'Agde houses a sprawling naturist village where summer months bring weekly festivals, yoga sessions, and body painting workshops. Visitors from all continents come together, fostering an international community spirit underpinned by mutual respect and the joys of freedom.

Further north in Germany, the *International Naturist Pentecost Meeting* attracts thousands of naturists from across Europe, hosted by dedicated naturist associations. These events aren't merely about being nude; they encompass a range of activities such as guided nature walks, volleyball tournaments, and communal dining experiences. Here, the notion of naturism melds seamlessly with an appreciation for nature, athleticism, and social interaction.

Across the Atlantic, America's clothing-optional festivals are as diverse as the country itself. The *American Association for Nude Recreation* (AANR) organizes a myriad of events throughout the year, from midsummer jubilation to autumnal retreats. One such celebration, the AANR SunFest, is a week-long extravaganza held in Florida, featuring live music, talent shows, and family activities. This festival particularly underscores the inclusive nature of naturism, welcoming families with children to experience the freedom and fun that come with nudity.

An entirely different flavor of celebration can be found in Japan with its deeply rooted Onsen (hot spring) culture. While not always associated with Western perceptions of naturism, these communal baths have been integral to Japanese life for centuries. Once a year, festivities like the *Hadaka Matsuri* (Naked Festival) are held, where men, clad in barely-there loincloths, participate in traditional rites. This event, while deeply spiritual, also epitomizes communal acceptance of the unclothed body.

Moving south to the Caribbean, the island of Jamaica hosts the annual *Nude Week*. Sun-seekers gather at popular resorts like Hedonism II in Negril, transforming a laid-back beach experience into a lively festival atmosphere. Imagine days filled with sunbathing, pool parties, and reggae nights alongside bonfires on the sandy shores. It's a truly hedonistic enjoyment of life, sun, and sea.

South America isn't left behind in these celebrations. Brazil, for instance, holds *Naturata*, a festival dedicated to naturism that usually occurs on the pristine beaches of Bahia. Naturata blends the vibrant Brazilian culture with naturist principles. Participants engage in samba lessons, capoeira demonstrations, and beach soccer. The rhythm of bossa nova mingles with the sound of the waves, creating an atmosphere of breathtaking freedom and exuberance.

In Australia, naturist gatherings gain momentum with the *Annual Nude Olympics* on Maslin Beach, south of Adelaide. This uniquely Australian event features a quirky mix of events like sack races, frisbee tossing, and body painting competitions, all taking place in the balmy summer sun. The event attracts a vast and varied crowd, creating a jovial and welcoming environment for both veterans and newcomers to the naturist scene.

Naturism also celebrates solidarity and cultural tradition in Africa. In South Africa, the *South African Nudist Association* organizes events such as the *Annual Bare Bush Camp*. Nestled amidst the African wilderness, this festival emphasizes a close connection with nature through guided bushwalks, stargazing evenings, and communal braais (barbeques). The sense of community, freedom, and respect for nature is palpable, reaffirming a harmonious coexistence.

In India, the emergence of naturist events is relatively new but growing rapidly. Goa has started to host smaller gatherings that focus not only on being in the nude but also on spirituality and wellness. Yoga retreats and meditation sessions celebrate the human body in its most natural state, underscoring deeper connections with oneself and surroundings.

These festivals are not just about external celebration but also about internal reflection and acceptance. They provide a space where people can shed societal norms and embrace their individuality. Each event, be it in a bustling urban center or a serene beach, brings together a community that values freedom, respect, and physical and emotional liberation. The beauty of these gatherings lies in their diversity, reflecting a world that, in its differences, finds common ground in the human form and spirit.

How to Plan Your Visit

Planning a visit to naturist festivals and events involves a mix of anticipation and preparation, aiming to ensure that your experience is as seamless and enjoyable as possible. First and foremost, familiarize yourself with the specific event you're interested in. Each festival has its own unique vibe, themes, and dress codes—even within the world of naturism. Researching beforehand can spare you any surprises and help you pack accordingly.

One of the initial steps is securing your tickets. Many naturist festivals are popular and sell out quickly. Check the event's official website regularly for updates on ticket sales and any package deals they might offer. Early bird tickets often come at a discount, so it's worth booking ahead of time. Make sure to note any deadlines or cutoffs for ticket purchases to avoid disappointment.

Accommodations are another critical element to consider well in advance. While some festivals offer camping options on-site, others might be near hotels or resorts. If you're opting for camping, ensure that you have a reliable tent, sleeping bag, and other camping essentials that align with naturist principles. For hotel stays, look into naturist-friendly accommodations or those in close proximity to the event. Some festivals also provide shuttles between suggested hotels and the event site.

Transportation to and from the event can vary dramatically based on your destination. Whether you're flying, driving, or taking public transportation, be sure to plan the route in advance. For international festivals, checking travel restrictions and visa requirements is a must. Remember to coordinate arrival and departure times with the festival schedule to maximize your experience.

Community engagement is a notable aspect of naturist festivals. Many events have social media groups or forums where you can connect with other attendees before the event. Joining these groups can provide valuable insights, tips, and even companionship for solo travelers. Engaging with the community beforehand also helps build excitement and allows you to ask questions directly to seasoned festival-goers.

Packing for a naturist festival involves more than just swimsuits and sunscreen. Since you'll be spending much of your time in the nude, focus more on comfort and convenience rather than fashion. Don't forget essentials like a good-quality sunblock, insect repellent, and comfortable footwear. A sarong or lightweight towel can be handy for when you need to sit on communal surfaces. Additionally, bring a reusable water bottle to stay hydrated, as naturist festivals often emphasize sustainability.

Understanding the weather conditions of your festival's location is crucial. Naturist events are typically held in pleasant climates, but weather can be unpredictable. Pack lightweight clothing for the day and warmer layers for the evening. Items like hats and sunglasses are also important for sun protection. If your festival is by the beach, consider bringing polarized sunglasses to reduce glare.

Health and hygiene shouldn't be overlooked. Even though you're embracing a more natural lifestyle, basic hygiene practices remain essential. Carry travel-sized toiletries, a small first-aid kit, and any personal medication you might need. Many festivals have communal showers and bathrooms, so a pair of flip-flops, biodegradable soap, and a quick-dry towel will prove useful. Keeping yourself clean and comfortable will enhance your overall experience.

Familiarize yourself with the festival's schedule and events. Naturist festivals often offer a range of activities, from yoga sessions and body painting to workshops and live music. Create a personalized itinerary that allows you to participate in your preferred events while also leaving room for spontaneous fun. Balancing structured activities with downtime can help you avoid feeling overwhelmed.

Etiquette is an important consideration at naturist festivals. Respecting personal space and consent is paramount. Always ask for permission before taking photographs that include other people, and be mindful of areas designated as camera-free zones. Stay aware of and adhere to the festival's rules regarding behavior, substance use, and even disposal of trash. This communal responsibility ensures a respectful and enjoyable experience for all attendees.

Financial planning is another aspect that shouldn't be underestimated. While some festivals have all-inclusive tickets, others may require additional payments for specific activities or amenities. Carry cash as well as cards, as some smaller vendors may not accept digital payments. Budget for your meals, souvenirs, and any impromptu experiences that may come up. It's wise to have a contingency fund for unexpected needs or emergencies.

Connecting with the culture of the festival's location can enrich your experience. If you're attending an international naturist festival, learning about local customs, language basics, and culinary delights can add a deeper layer of enjoyment to your trip. Immerse yourself in the surroundings and interact with locals when possible – it often leads to unforgettable moments and new friendships.

Lastly, mental preparation is just as important as the physical. Embracing naturism, especially in a group setting, requires a positive and open mindset. Take some time to reflect on your intentions for attending the festival and what you hope to gain from it. Cultivating a sense of acceptance, curiosity, and openness will contribute greatly to how you experience the event.

In summary, planning your visit to naturist festivals and events involves a multi-faceted approach, combining logistical planning with a mental and emotional readiness. By addressing these aspects thoroughly, you'll be primed for an unforgettable and liberating adventure that celebrates the naturist lifestyle. Each step, from securing tickets to packing essentials and understanding local etiquette, contributes to a holistic and fulfilling festival experience.

Chapter 22:
The Future of Naturist Travel

The future of naturist travel holds a tapestry of exciting possibilities and trends, blending innovation with tradition. Emerging destinations across the globe are warming up to the ethos of naturism, offering more varied and unique experiences. With a growing emphasis on sustainability, naturist resorts are incorporating eco-friendly practices and supporting local communities, making ethical travel more accessible. Technological advancements are set to enhance booking processes and tailor experiences to individual preferences. As cultural acceptance of naturism grows, the integration of wellness trends like naturist yoga and meditation retreats continue to gain momentum. Brace yourself for a world where the barriers are continually broken down, enhancing the liberating feeling of being one with nature in places yet to be explored.

Emerging Destinations

As naturism continues to evolve and grow globally, so too do the number of destinations that embrace this liberating lifestyle. New and exciting locales are emerging, offering naturists fresh and unexplored frontiers to consider for their next journey. These destinations range from isolated beaches in under-the-radar regions to burgeoning naturist-friendly cultures in places where such an idea may have once seemed far-fetched.

One such destination making waves is Eastern Europe. While Croatia has long been famous for its naturist resorts and stunning Adriatic coastline, other countries in the region are beginning to attract attention. Bulgaria, with its beautiful Black Sea coast, is quickly becoming a hotspot for naturists seeking a less commercialized, more intimate experience. Varna and Sozopol, with their charming old towns and pristine beaches, exemplify the allure of this emerging naturist haven.

On the opposite side of the globe, Asia is witnessing a quiet revolution in naturist travel. India, traditionally conservative regarding nudity, is showing pockets of transformation. Goa's laid-back attitude is no longer confined to its famed full-moon parties and yoga retreats; naturist-friendly areas are cropping up, inviting travelers to enjoy the serene beaches in their most natural state. Similarly, Thailand, already celebrated for its exotic and hospitable environment, offers hidden retreats in places like Koh Lanta and Koh Phangan, fostering a budding naturist scene.

But it's not just about new beaches or resorts opening up; it's about entire cultures beginning to accept and even celebrate the naturist philosophy. For instance, South Africa, known for its diverse landscapes and wildlife, is embracing naturism in unexpected ways. The Western Cape and KwaZulu-Natal regions are not only promoting traditional textiles as part of local culture but also recognizing naturism as a way to attract a more varied tourist demographic, thus broadening their hospitality horizons.

Shifting our gaze to the Middle East, naturism is finding a foothold in places once deemed unimaginable for such a lifestyle. Israel, with its progressive mindset and diverse population, offers secluded stretches along its Mediterranean coast where naturists can unwind away from the bustling cities. Turkey too, with its rich history and stunning coastline, is opening up to naturist communities. The Lycian coast, known for its azure waters and rugged beauty, is particularly promising as a naturist destination, blending the mystical allure of ancient ruins with the simplicity of a naturist retreat.

Australia and New Zealand, already known for their stunning naturist-friendly spots, continue to expand their offerings. Beyond Sydney's familiar surroundings, new pockets are sprouting up in Tasmania and along the rugged coasts of Western Australia. New Zealand's South Island, with its dramatic landscapes, provides ample solitude for naturists looking to connect with nature on a deeper level. In places like Abel Tasman and Fiordland, the blend of pristine wilderness and naturist ideals is creating uniquely immersive experiences.

Africa, a continent rich in natural beauty and cultural diversity, is another region witnessing a burgeoning naturist movement. Aside from South Africa, countries like Namibia are joining the conversation. With its vast, otherworldly landscapes, Namibia offers naturists a rare opportunity to experience the solitude of the desert and the wild beauty of places like Sossusvlei and Etosha. These emerging destinations provide not only a sense of liberation but also a profound connection to nature seldom felt elsewhere.

The Caribbean, already synonymous with naturist paradise, is revealing new gems beyond the popular spots in Jamaica and St. Martin. Lesser-known islands like Dominica and Grenada are stepping into the spotlight, inviting naturists to explore their unspoiled beaches and lush landscapes. In these tranquil corners of the Caribbean, the focus is on sustainability and preserving the natural environment, making them appealing for those who wish to minimize their ecological footprint while enjoying a naturist lifestyle.

In Europe, places like Estonia and Latvia are challenging the traditional naturist destinations' dominance. These Baltic States, with their enigmatic mix of medieval charm and untouched nature, offer serene and less commercialized environments for naturists. Coastal areas near the Gulf of Riga and the islands off Estonia's coast provide enticing, tranquil locales for naturist retreats, emphasizing a reconnection with nature amid northern Europe's distinct beauty.

Advancements in technology are also fostering new types of naturist experiences. Remote working trends and digital nomad culture now allow naturist travelers to blend work and leisure seamlessly. Naturist co-living spaces and eco-villages are popping up in innovative projects across the globe, from the lush landscapes of Costa Rica to the secluded areas in Portugal. These developments represent a move toward a holistic, sustainable lifestyle that integrates work, community, and naturism.

Additionally, naturist cruise lines are continuing to expand their routes, often discovering new ports of call that might surprise even the most seasoned travelers. Voyages through the less-traveled waters of Southeast Asia or the rugged coasts of South America offer not just a journey of discovery but also a floating haven for naturists to experience a sense of freedom while exploring new cultures and environments.

This renaissance of naturist travel isn't just about finding new beaches or trails; it's about a global shift toward acceptance and celebration of a lifestyle that values body positivity, environmental respect, and a profound connection to nature. Each emerging destination offers its unique take on what it means to embrace naturism, from the tranquil shores of India's Kerala to the wild landscapes of Namibia, each inviting travelers to shed not just their clothes but their inhibitions and societal constraints.

In essence, the future of naturist travel seems vibrant and dynamic, with emerging destinations promising new horizons and experiences that align with the core values of naturism. Whether you are seeking a serene coastal retreat, a rugged wilderness adventure, or a blend of culture and nature, these nascent spots on the map offer a wealth of opportunities to explore the world and yourself in the most natural way possible. The journey is no longer just about where you go, but how deeply you can connect with the essence of naturism in these captivating locales.

Trends and Innovations

Naturist travel is evolving, adapting to the changing times and the increasingly diverse needs of those who embrace this liberating lifestyle. The future of naturist travel is shaped by several key trends and innovations that pave the way for more inclusive, sustainable, and technologically integrated experiences. To understand these emerging patterns, we need to delve into the main elements that are driving these changes.

One of the most significant trends in naturist travel is the growing demand for inclusive and body-positive environments. Traditional naturist destinations often focus on creating a space where individuals can feel free from judgment and societal pressures. The future will likely see this ethos expand to include not just body acceptance but also diversity in all forms—whether that means accommodating different age groups, ethnic backgrounds, or levels of physical ability. Resorts and travel packages are increasingly incorporating activities and amenities designed to cater to a wider demographic, ensuring that everyone feels welcome and comfortable.

Sustainability is another pivotal trend that is shaping naturist destinations. As awareness of environmental issues increases, there's a growing desire among naturist travelers to minimize their ecological footprint. This means that many naturist resorts are investing in green technologies such as solar power, water recycling systems, and organic farming methods to provide eco-friendly accommodations. Guests can expect to participate in activities that emphasize environmental stewardship, such as beach clean-ups, tree planting, and educational workshops on sustainable living. The combination of naturism's inherent closeness to nature and a conscious effort towards sustainability makes this an exciting time for eco-conscious travelers.

Technology, too, is playing a fundamental role in the modernization of naturist travel. Enhanced connectivity and digital platforms are making it easier for naturists to find and communicate with each other. Mobile apps and online communities provide comprehensive directories of naturist-friendly locations, allowing travelers to plan their trips with ease. Virtual reality (VR) tours of accommodations and destinations can give potential visitors a realistic preview, setting accurate expectations and reducing any anxiety about their first naturist experience. Moreover, wearable technology like health monitors is being integrated into wellness programs at naturist resorts, offering personalized experiences that cater to individual health and fitness needs.

Social media is transforming how people perceive and engage with naturism. Platforms like Instagram, TikTok, and YouTube are being used by naturist influencers to share their journeys, breaking down misconceptions and promoting the naturist lifestyle to a broader audience. This increased visibility helps demystify naturism, encouraging more people to consider it as a viable travel option. Resorts and communities are also using social media to engage with younger generations, ensuring that naturist travel doesn't become a relic of the past but continues to thrive in contemporary culture.

Alongside technological and social media advancements, there's also a significant shift towards personalized and unique travel experiences. Traditional naturist resorts with their standard amenities are evolving to offer bespoke experiences tailored to individual tastes. Customizable travel packages that combine naturism with niche interests like art retreats, culinary tours, or adventure sports are gaining popularity. These specialized offerings cater to the growing demand for vacations that go beyond mere relaxation, providing enriching experiences that resonate on a deeper level.

Another exciting development is the rise of pop-up and temporary naturist events. These events, which can range from weekend getaways to week-long festivals, offer a dynamic and flexible alternative to traditional, permanent resorts. By utilizing beautiful natural locations such as secluded beaches, forests, and meadows, these pop-up events create a unique and ephemeral experience that feels fresh and spontaneous. Attendees can immerse themselves in a range of activities like yoga, workshops, live music, and communal dining, all while enjoying the freedom of naturism in a breathtaking setting.

Naturist travel is also becoming more integrated with wellness and holistic health practices. Many resorts are broadening their scope to include various wellness programs such as naturist yoga, meditation retreats, and spa treatments. These programs recognize the interconnectedness of physical, mental, and spiritual health, offering visitors a holistic approach to well-being. In the future, we can expect to see more collaboration with wellness professionals and an expansion of health-focused amenities, making naturist travel a comprehensive experience for rejuvenation.

Changes in societal attitudes towards naturism are also playing a crucial role in shaping its future. As mainstream acceptance of body positivity and natural living grows, naturist travel is increasingly seen as a legitimate and appealing choice. This change is reflected in the expanding media representation and the endorsement by influential figures and celebrities. Public awareness campaigns and education initiatives continue to dispel myths and normalize naturism, paving the way for broader acceptance and integration into mainstream travel options.

The defense and expansion of legal rights for naturists are critical aspects of the future landscape. Advocacy groups work tirelessly to protect the freedoms and rights of naturists, lobbying for legal recognition and protection of naturist spaces. We can anticipate more legally recognized naturist areas, which in turn encourage the development of new destinations and facilities. Legal clarity not only benefits seasoned naturists but also reassures newcomers by providing clear guidelines and protections, thus fostering a safe and welcoming environment.

Moreover, partnerships between naturist communities and local businesses are growing. These partnerships are crucial for supporting local economies and promoting cultural exchange. By involving local artisans, restaurants, and service providers, naturist destinations can offer authentic experiences that highlight regional culture and traditions. This collaboration is mutually beneficial: it supports small businesses while providing travelers with genuine and enriching interactions with the local culture.

In conclusion, the future of naturist travel is bright and full of possibilities. The trends and innovations emerging today reflect a blend of tradition and modernity, balancing the timeless appeal of naturism with contemporary advancements. Inclusive and body-positive environments, sustainable practices, technological integration, social media influence, personalized experiences, pop-up events, wellness programs, evolving societal attitudes, legal advocacy, and local partnerships are all key elements that are driving this transformative evolution. As naturist travel continues to grow and adapt, it promises a future of enriching, liberating, and unforgettable experiences for all who choose to embrace this unique way of traveling.

Conclusion

As we draw the curtains on this exploration of naturist travel, what we've uncovered is more than a mere list of vacation spots. We've delved into a lifestyle — a philosophy that embraces freedom, self-acceptance, and a closer connection to nature. Through the diverse landscapes we've traversed — from the pristine beaches of the Caribbean to the rugged coastlines of Oceania — the central theme remains the same: naturism is about more than nudity; it's about liberating oneself from societal norms and connecting with the world around us.

The journey we've embarked upon has taken us to lush rainforests, serene desert escapes, and cosmopolitan hotspots where naturism is seamlessly integrated into local culture. Each destination offered its unique flavor, whether it was the tranquil charm of British Columbia's hidden retreats or the vivacious spirit of Cap d'Agde in France. These sites serve as testaments to the diverse ways that naturist ideals can be embraced and celebrated across the globe.

One of the most compelling aspects of naturist travel is its ability to build a sense of community. Far from being solitary, naturism often fosters deep connections among like-minded individuals. The shared experience of baring it all, quite literally, lays the foundation for friendships that transcend traditional social barriers. In this sense, naturist travel isn't just about individual liberation; it's also about collective celebration.

However, our exploration hasn't shied away from addressing the practicalities and nuances of naturist travel. From packing essentials and understanding legalities to navigating the often complicated web of cultural expectations, we've covered the myriad aspects that make for a successful naturist adventure. Armed with this knowledge, you're better equipped to plan your journeys with confidence and ease.

We've also touched upon the increasingly crucial issue of sustainable travel. In a world grappling with environmental crises, it's more important than ever that our travel choices reflect a commitment to preserving the beauty we seek to enjoy. Naturism and sustainability go hand in hand, as both advocate for a lifestyle that is in harmony with nature.

Furthermore, the mental and physical wellness benefits of naturism cannot be overstated. The simplicity of returning to nature and shedding the constraints of clothing can lead to incredible improvements in mental clarity, stress reduction, and overall well-being. Engaging in activities such as naturist yoga and meditation only amplifies these benefits, providing a holistic approach to health that modern life often overlooks.

For families considering naturist vacations, the journey is a gateway to teaching children about body positivity and respect for natural environments. Family-friendly naturist destinations offer safe and fun environments where everyone, regardless of age, can enjoy the liberating experience of naturist living. Similarly, solo travelers find empowerment and confidence in navigating new environments alone, while groups discover extensive opportunities for socializing and shared experiences.

Naturism's unique appeal lies in its timelessness. Though it may adapt and evolve, its core principles remain unwavering — promoting sincerity, respect, and a profound appreciation for nature. As we look to the future, emerging destinations and innovative travel trends promise to broaden the horizons of naturist travel even further. Whether it's space travel or virtual reality experiences, the possibilities are as endless as they are exciting.

So, where do we go from here? Our exploration might end here, but your journey is just beginning. Take the knowledge and inspiration you've garnered from these pages, and let it fuel your own adventures. Whether it's a secluded beach in the Mediterranean or a naturist festival in South America, there's always a new corner of the world waiting to be discovered, a new place to embrace the liberating ethos of naturism.

Traveling as a naturist offers a unique lens through which to view the world. It's an invitation to see beyond the surface, to appreciate beauty in its most unadorned form, and to connect deeply with both nature and fellow travelers. The destinations we've covered provide a starting point, but the spirit of naturism is universal and can be practiced wherever you find yourself.

Naturist travel is as much about the inner journey as it is about the external. It's about peeling back the layers to uncover a simpler, more authentic way of being. By embracing naturism, you embark on a path of self-discovery and rejuvenation, finding freedom not just in travel, but in every aspect of life.

In closing, may you journey with an open heart and a liberated spirit. The world of naturist travel is vast and varied, filled with intriguing cultures, awe-inspiring landscapes, and welcoming communities. Here's to embracing the freedom, the adventure, and the limitless possibilities that lie ahead.

Appendix A:
Appendix

The appendix serves as a comprehensive resource for additional information that will enhance your naturist travel experiences. Here, you'll find a curated list of invaluable contacts, essential websites, and forums dedicated to naturist travel. These resources are designed to offer you ongoing support and advice, ensuring that every aspect of your journey is well-informed and enjoyable. Whether you're seeking detailed maps, reading personal travel stories from fellow naturists, or looking for the latest updates on naturist events, this section is your go-to guide for a seamless and enriching adventure.

Resources and Contacts

When embarking on a naturist journey, having a curated list of resources and contacts can transform your experience from ordinary to extraordinary. It's these connections that provide insider tips, help you navigate unfamiliar territories, and offer reassurance in moments of uncertainty. The naturist world, after all, is as much about community as it is about freedom and exploration. Here, you'll find a carefully compiled list to help you immerse yourself seamlessly into naturist travel.

First and foremost, naturist organizations are invaluable resources. The American Association for Nude Recreation (AANR) and the Federation of Canadian Naturists (FCN) are excellent points of contact for North American travelers. Both organizations offer extensive information about naturist resorts, legalities, and events within their regions. Whether you're looking for year-round resorts or seasonal gatherings, these groups can guide you to hidden gems and well-established naturist hot spots.

For those venturing to Europe, the International Naturist Federation (INF) stands as a beacon. With a network stretching across countries like France, Spain, and the Netherlands, the INF can connect you with local clubs and events that might otherwise fly under the radar. The Naturist Association Switzerland (NATUR) and the British Naturism organization also fall under the INF umbrella, making it easier to plan multiple stops across the continent.

Connecting with local naturist clubs can enrich your travels profoundly. These clubs often host social events, provide educational workshops, and sometimes even offer accommodation. Consider reaching out to the Southern California Naturist Association (SCNA) or the Naturist Society of Ireland before you travel. They can offer personalized advice, introduce you to local members, and even organize meet-ups to make your trip more memorable.

Naturist forums and websites serve as digital town squares for enthusiasts around the globe. Popular platforms like *NaturistPlace* and *TrueNudists* offer forums where you can ask questions, share experiences, and get recommendations from seasoned travelers. You can find threads discussing everything from the best nude beaches in Thailand to tips for first-time nude cruisers. These forums are a great way to do pre-trip research and even make friends before setting foot on your journey.

Social media also plays a significant role in the naturist community, fostering connections through groups and pages dedicated to naturist living and travel. Platforms like Facebook and Instagram feature vibrant naturist communities. Pages like "Naturist Travel" and "Barefoot Life" often post about events, tips, and new destinations. Joining these groups can keep you updated with the latest trends and help you stay connected with fellow naturists worldwide.

For those interested in specialized travel experiences like naturist cruises or festivals, niche travel agencies can be a godsend. Companies like Bare Necessities and Nakation specialize in organizing naturist cruises that traverse the Caribbean, Mediterranean, and even South Pacific. Their expertise allows you to relax, knowing that every detail—from destinations to activities—is catered to the naturist lifestyle.

Another excellent resource is the naturist campsite directory available through platforms like Camping Naturist. This site lists a plethora of naturist campsites throughout Europe, providing reviews, amenities, and booking options. Whether you're looking for a peaceful retreat in the South of France or a social camping ground in Croatia, this directory helps you find the perfect spot to pitch your tent.

It's also advisable to carry a list of emergency contacts pertinent to your destination. Local embassies, healthcare facilities familiar with treating foreigners, and even trusted local guides can serve as useful lifelines. Websites like Travel.state.gov and its equivalents in other countries often have updated contact information and travel advisories, which can be crucial in navigating unexpected situations.

Don't overlook the benefits of travel insurance, especially policies that cater to naturist travel. Companies like World Nomads offer customizable policies that include coverage for naturist activities. Their 24-hour support lines are beneficial, providing peace of mind when you're exploring new frontiers.

For naturists traveling with families, specialized forums and websites can offer invaluable support. Looking for the best child-friendly naturist resorts or tips on educating young ones about naturism? Websites like *Family Naturist Travel* and *KidNaturists* provide insights and advice tailored to family-oriented naturist vacations. They offer forums for parents, lists of kid-friendly resorts, and even packing tips for children.

The world of naturist travel is rich and varied, and tapping into these resources and contacts can make a significant difference. By reaching out to these organizations, forums, and agencies, you arm yourself with knowledge and support that transforms your journey into an unforgettable, liberating experience. Let's step into this world of freedom and adventure confidently, knowing that a community is always there to guide you.

Helpful Websites and Forums

In the expansive world of naturist travel, online resources play a pivotal role in guiding enthusiasts to new and exciting destinations. Particularly useful are websites and forums dedicated to naturism, offering a wealth of information, personal experiences, and community support for both novice and seasoned naturists. By tapping into these digital spaces, one can find up-to-date insights about travel locations, legalities, social aspects, and many other nuances that come with naturist travel.

One of the most renowned websites for naturist travelers is *NaturistDirectory.com*. It serves as a comprehensive guide to naturist resorts, beaches, and events worldwide. Not only does it provide detailed descriptions of destinations, but it also includes reviews and ratings from other naturists. This makes it easier to gauge what to expect and decide which places might suit one's preferences best.

TripAdvisor's Traveler Forums have dedicated sections and threads where naturist travelers share their insights and experiences. These forums can be particularly helpful when seeking first-hand accounts of naturist destinations and practical advice on what to bring or expect. Additionally, they often include tips on local customs and etiquette, crucial for anyone looking to immerse themselves respectfully into different cultures.

Another excellent resource is *NakedWanderings.com*, a blog and forum run by passionate naturists who document their travels around the globe. Their site features detailed articles and stunning photography that vividly capture the essence of naturist life and travel. The accompanying forums allow for engaging discussions where travelers can ask for advice, share experiences, and connect with like-minded individuals.

Reddit also hosts several communities focused on naturism, such as r/naturism and r/nudism. These subreddit forums are invaluable for candid discussions and diverse perspectives on naturist travel. Users frequently share unique spots and lesser-known destinations, making these forums a goldmine for discovering hidden gems.

One cannot overlook the support and information provided by the **International Naturist Federation (INF)**. Their official website not only lists affiliated naturist resorts and clubs around the world but also provides updates on international naturist events. Membership in INF often grants access to additional resources and discounts, enhancing the overall travel experience.

For naturist travel specifically in the United States, the *American Association for Nude Recreation (AANR)* offers a wealth of information. Their website includes a directory of affiliated clubs and resorts, as well as resources on legal considerations and upcoming naturist events in North America. This can be particularly useful for planning a vacation that aligns with one of these social gatherings.

If you're venturing into Europe, **NaturistBnB** is an innovative platform similar to Airbnb but tailored for naturists. It lists clothing-optional accommodations in various countries, making it easier to find naturist-friendly places to stay. This platform ensures that travelers can enjoy their naturist lifestyle even during their downtime, away from the beaches and resorts.

FreedomIsEverything is another compelling blog and forum that maps out the journey of full-time naturists. This site is perfect for those considering long-term or more extensive naturist travels. It offers tips on sustainable travel practices, budget considerations, and maintaining a naturist lifestyle on the road.

For naturist travel planning, *ClothingOptionalTrips.com* stands out as a specialized travel agency focused on organizing trips to naturist destinations. They cover everything from booking and itineraries to personalized travel advice, ensuring a hassle-free and enjoyable journey. Engaging with such agencies can take the guesswork out of travel planning, leaving more time to enjoy the naturist experience fully.

Forums like **The Free Beach Day Support Group** are also invaluable, offering a community-driven perspective on naturist travel. Participants discuss their visits to various free beaches and provide practical advice on access, amenities, and the overall vibe. This can be particularly beneficial for those uncertain about visiting a new or lesser-known naturist spot.

Another key resource is the *TravelNaturist.com* website, which features a blend of expert advice and user-generated content. This site includes destination reviews, packing lists, legal advice, and cultural tips for naturist travelers. The user-generated component allows travelers to share their stories and experiences, enriching the site with diverse and authentic insights.

Additionally, Facebook groups such as **Worldwide Naturists** and **Free in Nature** offer dynamic platforms for interaction. These groups are places where naturists from across the globe share photos, travel tips, and stories. They often organize meetups and events, providing real-world opportunities to connect with fellow naturists.

One cannot overlook the abundance of information found on *Yelp*. While not exclusively for naturists, Yelp reviews often include experiences at clothing-optional beaches and resorts. Reading through these reviews can provide additional, localized insights into the destinations listed on more specialized websites.

Finally, websites like **Green Naturist** blend naturist travel with eco-friendly practices. This site emphasizes sustainable and ethical naturist travel, offering tips on how to minimize environmental impact while enjoying naturist activities. This resource is ideal for those who wish to align their love for naturism with a commitment to environmental stewardship.

In sum, these websites and forums are not just about finding places to visit; they create a sense of community and shared discovery. They offer practical advice, cultural insights, and first-hand experiences that enrich the journey of a naturist traveler. By engaging with these resources, one can embark on naturist adventures that are not only liberating but also deeply informed and connected to a global network of like-minded individuals.

Printed in Great Britain
by Amazon

57334796R00128